THE SCOTLAND OF OUR SONS

'They helped every one his neighbour ; and every one said to his brother, Be of good courage.

' So the carpenter encouraged the goldsmith, and he that smootheth with the hammer him that smote the anvil, saying, It is ready for the sodering : and he fastened it with nails, that it should not be moved.'

A WEST HIGHLAND GLEN

Potential site for a community getting a living
from fishing, stock rearing on the hill, with
fruit and vegetable growing, pigs and poultry
keeping in the fertile alluvial plain.

THE SCOTLAND OF OUR SONS

BY

ALEXANDER MACLEHOSE

With two chapters by
SIR JOHN ORR
Director of the Rowett Research Institute
Aberdeen

LONDON
ALEXANDER MACLEHOSE & CO.
58 BLOOMSBURY STREET
1937

PRINTED IN GREAT BRITAIN BY ROBERT MACLEHOSE AND CO. LTD.
THE UNIVERSITY PRESS, GLASGOW

TO
E. H. B.

PREFACE

THIS IS an age of planning. Plans in democratic countries often break down because they do not grip the imagination of the people who have to work them. This is especially true of Scotland. Many plans have been put forward for Scotland, but the lack of a national enthusiasm has prevented them from being so fruitful as they would otherwise have been.

This book is intended to tap some of the enthusiasm which lies not far below the surface of the national character, and to suggest ways in which a sturdy patriotism can put itself to immediate and practical use. The reader is referred in particular to Chapter VI, where Sir John Orr discusses ' Scotland as it might be '.

I have received help in writing this book

from many people, to all of whom I am most grateful. Mr. Robert Hurd, a Scottish Nationalist, has given me many frank comments and much useful information ; Mr. L. E. G. Laughton, of the Carnegie United Kingdom Trust, assisted me in the chapter on Rural Amenities, and Mr. Ian Macpherson in that on Rural Industries ; Sir John Sutherland, Mr. Edward Shiels, Mr. J. L. Campbell and Mr. Iverach McDonald have also given me valuable help.

To Sir John Orr, Director of the Rowett Research Institute, Aberdeen, who has made a special study of nutrition problems, I am much indebted for the two constructive chapters that he has kindly written for this book.

I have to thank Mr. Hugh Quigley for allowing me to reproduce a quotation on water-power schemes from *A Plan for the Highlands* (Methuen) and Professor R. G. Stapledon and Messrs. Faber and Faber for permission to print three passages from *The*

PREFACE

Land Now and To-morrow and *The Hill Lands of Britain*.

The figures on page 19 are taken, by permission of the Editor of *Planning*, from the broadsheet on the Highlands published by PEP on September 8th, 1936. It is encouraging to note from the latest Report of the Registrar-General that the rise in Scotland's population since the Census of 1931 still continues.

A. M.

LAMINGTON,
    October, 1937.

CONTENTS

*The frontispiece illustration is from a
photograph by Robert M. Adam*

xi

of our present book, will be intelligible if we remind ourselves who King James was and what he did.

He was a man in whom many contraries met. It was his wedding to Henry VII's daughter that at last united, ninety years after his death, the Crowns of Scotland and England and brought peace to two countries that had fought each other, off and on, for three hundred years: and yet James himself was the only King of Scotland to die in battle against the English.[1] His marriage was loveless, arranged to suit his country's interests, and took place a few months after the true love of his chequered life, a beautiful girl called Margaret Drummond, had died of poison. The jealousy of his nobles had prevented him from marrying the woman he loved, yet he bowed himself to the people's will and carried on with a heavy heart. He caused masses to be said daily for the peace of his lady's soul,

[1] Except Malcolm Canmore (d. 1093), who also married an English Princess.

and the first encounter with his future wife points a painful contrast between love and duty.

Here, as throughout his life, what united the conflicting elements of his mind and guided his decision, was the knowledge of what he owed to Scotland as her King. He was, almost more truly than any King of either Scotland or England until his descendant George V, the father of his people. He lived before the days of ' constitutional ' monarchy, and this fatherhood involved him in constant personal leadership. Wherever he went in Scotland, he was both his country's human image and the spear-point of all her decisions, in peace or war. This position he won, much less by heredity (the same could never have been said of his father, James III) than by the loyalty which he inspired in all classes of his subjects, Lowland and Highland, so that they found in him a bond of unity such as no Scottish King had been to his people since the days of Bruce, nearly two centuries before.

Both the Puritanism of the Reformers and the gay *joie de vivre* of his grand-daughter Queen Mary were represented in James IV. He made long pilgrimages of repentance to St. Ninian's shrine at Whithorn and other holy places in Scotland—pilgrimages none the less sincere that he would sometimes visit one of his sweethearts on the way. The Scottish character is complex, and its complexity not seldom shows itself in such ways as these, so unlike the Pharisees who would neither dance nor mourn. The Scots do both at once, and James was our true prototype. But since his death we have fallen upon a grave weakness. Though the national character still contains very striking opposites in its make-up, these opposite characteristics have tended to become specialised in different groups or sects in the nation, and with typical Scottish vehemence each sect believes, nay knows, itself to be right and its opponents damned. Self-righteousness has been always the prerogative rather of the Covenanters and their kind, partly because their outlook is narrower and they do not get to see much at all beyond the state of their own souls and, by vivid contrast, that of their opponents'. These, on the other hand, have usually had a wider vision, even though it might not be so earnest or profound. Our present purpose is fortunately not the impossible one of deciding which of the two parties was right, but to show how in James IV such contradictory tendencies could be harmonised and controlled. Consciously as well as unconsciously, in his people's life as in his own mind, he sought to achieve a balance, and a balance that offers the better example to us because it was not arrived at by pruning the more active impulses and enterprises of any one side of the national or the personal life, but rather by stimulating what needed encouragement, and forwarding a larger life within the whole nation.

His aim was to make Scotland a united country, at peace in itself, at peace with its neighbour England, and part also of a Christian

Europe herself at peace within her borders and united against the Moslem invader then advancing up the Danube. James alone could not achieve all this, and the selfish pride of many of the European monarchs—the Pope and Henry VIII included—set the Christian nations on fire among themselves, while the Turk was preparing to conquer Hungary at leisure. Nevertheless, in his first and principal purpose, James succeeded. He united Scotland. The old feuds of the nobles against the Crown, of Highland against Lowland, and the new clash between the rising merchants of the towns and the peasants on the land— all these were dissolved by a common loyalty to Scotland, in the person of the King whom all alike loved with an enthusiasm that was much more than formal, and involved a far greater sacrifice than any King nowadays could expect to claim. The expedition to Flodden was not popular. Scotland had no zeal for the King's quarrel, which was misjudged, and was probably a consequence of

nerves too heavily strained by anxiety for the
public weal, and no longer soothed as in his
earlier years by private happiness. But though
there was no good will to the war, every
able-bodied man assembled cheerfully at the
Borough Muir to the gathering, and no more
united army ever set out from Scotland in its
country's cause. When it came to the battle,
earls, bishops, knights and commoners went
down like snow before the English bills.
Scotland was out-generalled on that September day and the English weapons were the
more effective as the battle was fought, but
for sheer loyalty to a King who knew how
to die there is no date more glorious in
Scottish history.

Bruce would certainly have won Flodden.
James, for all his brilliant qualities, was an
amateur, and he not only allowed the English
to deprive him of the advantage of position,
but he failed to match his tactics with his
weapons. Bruce, who had the strength and
thoroughness of a professional, would have

seen to this. But Scotland has produced only
the one Bruce, and what concerns us here is
that James, in spite of some faults of temperament which must have been well known to
his people, yet won their full devotion and
banished discord from a country conspicuous
for its internal strife. This achievement,
though less spectacular, is more important for
us to remember now than the great disaster
of Flodden which brought it to an end, and
let the dogs of civil dissension loose again to
harry Scotland for four hundred years.

We are returning at last, under stress of
troubles, to a unity among ourselves. That
day has not actually come, but when it does,
his people's vision will have been fulfilled and
James IV will ride home. Certainly his spirit
is already alive, and his horse may be saddling
even now.

CHAPTER II

A BALANCED SCOTLAND

'And here was a child with the wine of the hills in his blood, the pride of princes, the purity of saints, the courage of heroes, the singing fire of poets, all coursing through his little being. And God help the child, what good was all that going to do him in the streets and buildings, in the holds of half-built ships, in the prisons of factories ? Would he not be happier there with the blood of a thousand slaves in his veins ? '

EDWARD SHIELS, *Gael over Glasgow*

SCOTLAND WILL never attain that balance between town and country which she needs for her well-being, until the Highlands and Islands have been re-peopled. We have seen how James IV tried to give his Kingdom a full, balanced and flourishing life, and neither he nor anyone who in these days undertakes the care of Scotland's interests can be content to see these potential homes of a virile race remain empty. In a later chapter we shall consider some of the particular advantages which will follow for Scotland when her glens and islands ring once more with the joyful cry of human voices no less than with the call of the birds who at present, outside the holiday season, practically have the place to themselves.

But before we can look forward to that time, we have first to study the problem of the Highlands in relation to Scotland's condition as a whole. It is all very well to plead that if one member suffers all the members suffer with it: there is another saying, ' If thine eye offend thee, pluck it out and cast it from thee.' This seems in practice (not yet officially) to be the attitude adopted towards the Highlands by the Government, and by certain business men from Glasgow who tell you with a gleaming eye, ' Scotland's all right. Don't you believe it if anyone says she's in a bad way. She's doing fine, old boy.' What they mean, of course, is that the trade returns show a marked improvement, especially in the heavy industries centred round Glasgow and the Clyde. Quite apart from the important question how far this boom in the Glasgow neighbourhood depends on the re-armament programme and to a large extent will stop when that stops, this kind of reasoning betrays an *unbalanced* view of Scotland as a whole, at a time when the Highlands are far from flourishing. Such a view may be natural to a contractor whose thoughts are wrapped up in steel, but would never be allowed to exercise the influence in Government circles that it unfortunately does at present, if Scotland were ruled by a monarch lifted, as James IV was lifted, above the sectional interests to which Scotland, left to itself, has always been too prone. We need a larger purpose to our lives if we are to re-shape our country as its well-being requires. It was just that larger purpose which the great Kings gave to Scotland, and which we have so sorely lacked ever since 1513.

The test of Kingship, as of all leadership, lies in its power to call out the greatness of the common man. The relation between King and people is mutual: the one acts on the other. Reviewing Miss Mackenzie's *Robert Bruce King of Scots*, William Power wrote: ' This inspiring book shows how our greatest King owed his greatness to his increasing reliance upon the common folk of Scotland, who had given countless proofs of their passionate loyalty to a real King of Scots.' This is excellently said. What the common folk of Scotland did once they would do again, even now, if they had the opportunity; and just as by giving Bruce a chance to prove his greatness they proved their own, and surprised England and the chivalry of Europe, so they would to-day astonish the prophets of despair who preach that Man will no longer respond except to that which feeds his animal instincts. From the material point of view, it must have paid the men who went to the wars with Wallace and ten years later with Bruce to allow the English peaceably to annex their castles and rule them with that rough and hearty justice which the Plantagenets were well accustomed to dispense. Taxation, even oppression, under such a rule could not have inflicted so much *economic* injury on Scotland as resulted from the wars and threats of war that harried us for three centuries. When we took up the English challenge in 1297, we knew that the price of freedom must be—not for that generation only, but during a future which no man could estimate—an unsleeping watch and the readiness at any hour to don a breastplate, go out from cottage or castle and perhaps never return. That was the price which our forefathers paid, or stood ready to pay, during three hundred years. What were they getting for it? They were no fools, and knew what they were about.

What they were getting, if we look below the surface, is the very thing which we are losing—freedom of the spirit. There is a freedom of the body—the freedom to eat and drink, to move (within limits) where one likes, to satisfy one's ordinary desires—and this freedom, as we saw, our ancestors might have obtained without difficulty under English rule. Any conqueror, any dictator, tries to let his subjects have as much of *this* kind of freedom as he can, for it keeps them contented and apt instruments to his own designs. It is precisely this kind of freedom that a sheep enjoys, being pastured, shepherded and fattened, until its totally unforeseen day of doom arrives, and it is sent (without the slightest power of resistance or choice of its own destiny) to the butcher. That is the end of a sheep, and the same will be the end of our own herd-minded, comfort-loving, bamboozled civilisation.

That is why it is so necessary for Scotland (what England may do is her own concern) to get its head, so to speak, above water again and to provide for its national life some outlet to the infinite horizon of the spirit. Such an outlet would be provided for all Scotland if the Highlands were restored to their proper place in the national life, as the home of men. What we need is much more than a recreational outlet for townspeople on week-ends and the summer holidays: it is to get the *balance* of our national life more evenly swung between town and country; at present, as everyone has to realise, the weight both of population and influence is heavily in favour of the towns. For reasons of physical health alone this state of affairs would not be desirable; in time of war, it would become doubly dangerous because of air-attack and a probable food-shortage; but, above all, it is this excessive urbanisation which is more and more robbing us of that one thing for which our ancestors sacrificed peace, comfort and life itself—the freedom of the spirit.

To say that Scotland is excessively urbanised is not to deny the towns their rightful importance in our life. They are clearly essential to Scotland's economy, and the only objection to them is that by neglect of our true interest we have allowed them to become swollen both in size and consequence. The drift to the towns is natural in a civilisation becoming increasingly mechanised, and this question of mechanisation and the growing herd-instinct must be reserved for special study later. It is part of modern life, and did not originate in Scotland whose people are naturally independent-minded, however skilled they may also be at the manipulation of machines.

But Scotland suffers from a still deeper disquiet. If Man has one fear more than another, it is the fear of losing himself. We were told, of course, by the Founder of our religion that the process might have great virtue, but we are on the whole not adventurous. It is this which contributes to the growth of the towns: people feel more at home in a herd; and, on a deeper level, it shows itself in the corresponding insecurity which nearly every individual now feels lest the machine with its infinite

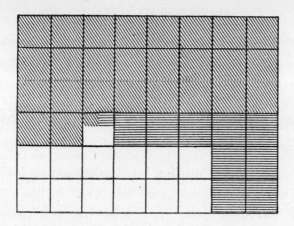

POPULATION OF SCOTLAND IN 1931

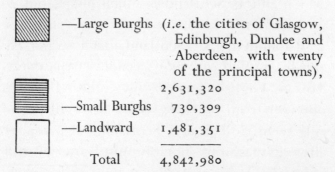

—Large Burghs (*i.e.* the cities of Glasgow, Edinburgh, Dundee and Aberdeen, with twenty of the principal towns), 2,631,320

—Small Burghs   730,309

—Landward   1,481,351
_____

Total   4,842,980

Out of every 20 people in Scotland fewer than 6 live in the country. The estimated population of Scotland as at 30th June, 1936, was 4,966,300, of whom 2,719,300 live in the large burghs, and 1,492,400 in rural districts.

possibilities of development may become master, and sweep him off the board altogether. We are like rabbits in a cornfield which the reaper is cutting on all four sides around us: we do not know which way to run.

Such uncertainties are common to the modern world, and may be cured in his own life by each individual if he cares to exert himself for the purpose. The deep disquiet which afflicts Scotland is much older, but it is the same in kind. It is the fear, only too well founded, that Scotland may lose herself and be snuffed out like a candle in the dark. To an Englishman or any other friendly observer from outside, such a fear will probably seem ridiculous. Scotland still prospers after its fashion, notably just now in the industrial belt, and the export of brains— always our choicest export—goes on.

Nevertheless the fact is there, that of the two ways of losing herself Scotland must soon choose one or the other. She can either

THE COURSE OF SCOTTISH AND HIGHLAND POPULATION

	Scotland	Northern Division (Kinross, Perth, Bute, Argyll and all counties northward, excluding Dundee City)		HIGHLANDS				Per cent. of Scotland			ISLANDS (included in foregoing)	
			Per cent. of Scotland	Urban	Rural	Total	Urban	Rural	Total			Per cent. of Scotland
1801....	1,608,420	740,597	46·0	—	—	—	—	—	—	—	—	—
1831....	2,364,386	949,793	40·2	—	—	—	—	—	—	—	—	—
1861....	3,062,294	1,020,115	33·3	111,586	402,354	513,940	3·6	13·1	16·8	164,994		5·4
1891....	4,025,647	1,070,077	26·6	142,582	343,969	486,551	3·5	8·5	12·1	159,899		4·0
1921....	4,882,497	1,046,208	21·4	153,185	298,171	451,356	3·1	6·1	9·2	154,588		3·2
1931....	4,842,980	979,195	20·2	140,474	273,531	414,005	2·9	5·6	8·5	124,796		2·6
1934....	4,934,000	984,280	19·9	—	—	412,222	—	—	8.35	—		—

POPULATION, AREA AND RATEABLE VALUE OF THE HIGHLANDS COMPARED WITH GREAT BRITAIN

	Population, 1934	Per cent.	Area 000 Acres	Per cent.	Rateable Value, 1933-34			
					£000	Per cent.	Per head	Per acre
							£ s.	£ s.
Perth and Inverness Burghs	58,241	—	5	—	507	—	—	0 3
Rest of Highlands	353,981	0·8	10,583	18·8	1,668	0·5	4 14	0 4
Total Highlands	412,222	0·9	10,588	18·8	2,175	0·7	5 5	0 4
Rest of Scotland	4,522,069	10·0	8,481	15·1	35,489	11·4	7 17	4 7
England and Wales	40,467,000	89·1	37,339	66·1	274,228	87·9	6 16	7 7
GREAT BRITAIN	45,401,000	100	56,408	100	311,892	100	6 17	5 10

continue to drift in the channel where she has been drifting for some time, losing all her characteristic features in an urban mentality which may be American in origin, but which follows the cinema as surely as trade follows the flag: losing her own human stock from the Highlands, and content to develop these instead as a recreation-ground whose principal attraction is the very fact that it *once* was the home of men worthy to live in it: losing the coherent influence which Scotland used to exert in the councils of Europe and subsequently at Westminster. All this is going, unless we make a united effort to redeem it. But all this could be won back, and more too, if we elect the other and nobler way of losing ourselves. ' He that loseth his life for My sake ', said Christ, ' shall find it.' We have no call at present to import religion into the argument. Religion, no doubt, is a part of all real life, but Scotland must stand on its own legs and rather invite a religious inspection of the results of its crusading effort when these are to show, than pretend that there is anything *specifically* religious in placing our sons in the land which the Lord their God gave them to inhabit.

The words quoted above, however, are not restricted only to the New Testament. They apply outside, and were so intended. And precisely in the mouth of a King, who is a real King to his people, they are appropriate. Well might Bruce have spoken such words before any of his great battles for Scotland's independence. His cause was pure, and his heart single. And our trouble to-day is that in the face of a need as great, we have no one who will rally us by a leadership so inspired. Only a King, or someone like a King, can do it. A party politician, even in a National Government, has to have one eye on the next election and perhaps also on the opinion of colleagues who are assessing that election with a view on some different stratum of voters. Even if the cause of such a Minister is pure, no one can believe that his heart is entirely single. He has the further handicap that those voters who belong to a party opposing his, will not be anxious to increase his prestige, and may therefore hold aloof from any call he may make to put the interests of Scotland before those of their class or party.

The Scottish Nationalists have attempted to get over this difficulty by starting a party all of whose members will put the interests of Scotland before anything else, and whose appeal to the Scottish people might therefore be supposed to be as pure as you could wish. Their appeal has been, in the matter of seats won at Westminster, entirely unsuccessful. In the world of politics it is necessary to be realist, and I do not think it was good sense to expect to detach voters from the two principal parties which, ever since the War, have stood for two quite opposing theories of government, theories that touch every single voter directly in the part where a voter is most naturally sensitive, his pocket. Whether you are a Scot, an Englishman or a Welshman, you are affected by this question of taxation, and you will not easily be dissuaded from lending your weight to the side you favour, by the appeal of a party whose maximum total number of *candidates* at any General Election has never exceeded seven. Into a political wilderness so unpromising, even Moses could not have persuaded the children of Israel.

The party's programme and ideas have looked as doctrinaire as the Socialist ideology, and to be founded less on a love of Scotland than on a dislike of England, of Conservatives and of all the powers that be. A friend of mine who has lived in the thick of it for years, who loves Scotland and has no roots either in England or in Conservatism, tells me that if you trace to their source many of the symbols hitherto most characteristic of the Scottish National Party, you will find ' a *personal* jealousy of the Englishman who rules the roost '. It would be ridiculous to suggest

that every individual member of the Party is
jealous of England, or that such a motive is
consciously active in the minds of its present
leaders. A certain justification for that opinion must, however, have been given in the
past, or the movement would have attracted
many more adherents than in fact it has.

You might take this as evidence of the
Scotsman's unique ability to disagree with
Scotsmen. Yet it is a fact that, once Scotsmen are banded together under a common
banner, nothing can disintegrate them; the
military record of our land shows that clearly
enough. Scotsmen disagree and break away
when there is no unifying force present, no
adequate leadership, no elemental, single
Purpose. The leaders of the National Party
have misunderstood their own countrymen,
and have either failed to supply that Purpose,
or have pitched it too low.

In the chapter on ' A Parliament in Scotland ' there will be more to say about the
Scottish Nationalists, and to consider whether

some of the men who speak in their name have spoken for the true Scotland, and not for a Little Scotland conceived in their own image. It is not so much a new party that we want, or a new set of measures to be passed into law, as new men and a new spirit within us. We need to recover the old faith of our forefathers, men who were afraid of nothing; our faith has sunk so far that we are afraid even of ourselves. Two remedies are open, neither facile and both essential: first, for each individual to remake his faith in lonely communion with the hills, or in any other place and way as he best likes; and secondly, when his purpose has been thus cleared, that in action he shall be as determined and tenacious as his fathers.

CHAPTER III

THE MASTER ISSUE

' The master issue is what human beings in the aggregate and individually will be up to, and that is more a matter of emotion than of muscle.'

R. G. STAPLEDON, *The Hill Lands of Britain*

SCOTLAND IS one and it is just for that reason that none of her provinces must be allowed to perish: of all these, the Highlands are in most immediate danger of dying. In the Middle Ages, before the twin inventions of the bullet and the ballot, quality counted. Now what counts is quantity, and the Highlander, who man for man is still as ' pretty a gentleman ' as you will find in all Britain, is become too scarce a breed to weigh against the swarming inhabitants of a modern city. As the Highlands in consequence lose prestige, so the Highlander, to whom the possession of prestige has always been a vital part of his spiritual food, tends to drift away from a land so forgotten, and the men and women who remain are beginning to lose heart. Let us help them while we have the power, or the night will come when it will be too late to help them.

Re-population of the Highlands is needed to restore the balance in Scotland, not only between town and country, but between Lowland and Highland. Sometimes you hear people suggesting that the Scottish Lowlander has more in common with a North of England man than he has with the Highlander, and that the cultural line between England and Scotland should be drawn along Antonine's wall, near Stirling, and not where the prudent Emperor Hadrian drew it, between Newcastle and Carlisle. This argument is based on the belief that the Celts are found only north of the ' Highland line '—a belief which does not square with the facts. For though the Scots, like the English, are now a very mixed race, yet strong traces of Celtic descent will be found in Galloway and on the Borders, and the Highlanders for their part have a good deal of Viking blood in them. The solidarity of Scotland rests in part on the Celtic ancestry from which every Scot is ultimately derived, but still more on the bond of history. Scotland is one of the few small countries in the world that have never been conquered.[1] Wales and Ireland fell to the English invader, but Scotland remained free, and the reason— which has influenced our history ever since— was that every district of Scotland—Lowlands, Highlands, the Eastern counties north of Forth, and the Western Isles—joined in the successful fight for freedom. Scotland became a nation under Wallace and Bruce, and she remains a nation to this day. There is less division of race or culture or senti-

---

[1] Both Edward I and Cromwell swept over Scotland with their armies and occupied the country, but very soon after they died Scotland became free. We have had plenty of national disasters and humiliations since those days; what we most suffer from just now is a lack of primitive energy and *guts*.

ment between the Scots who live south of the ' Highland line ' and those who live north of it, than you would find to-day between the inhabitants of Burgundy and Provence.

The Highlands have been a tremendous pillar in the Scottish temple, and if we allowed that pillar to crash, the temple itself would be in ruins. To many visitors, to many Scots even, the country north of Stirling is a mere play-ground of romance. Its proper and historic function is to be the home of men, as Scottish history down to the Union of the Crowns bears ample witness. Of the great lords who stood by Bruce at his crowning in 1306 and helped in the years that followed to make that symbolic act a coronation in deed and truth, all except James Douglas and the Bishop of Glasgow came from north of Forth. The Highlanders were devoted personally to Bruce, who commanded their division at the Battle of Bannockburn, and they renewed this loyalty to his two greatest successors, James II and James IV. Though during other reigns they were often found rebelling against the Crown, they were never insignificant, and to great leadership they never once failed to make a great response.

There is neither room nor occasion here to offer a summary of Highland history. Suffice it to say that anyone who looks into the records will find that the Highlands at all periods down to 1603 figure prominently in all that was done. After the King went to London, the part played by Highlanders becomes less regular and more romantic, and it is unfortunately this later and less typical period that is most familiar to English and American readers. The intense hatred felt for Montrose in Southern Scotland was due to his employment of Highlanders,[1] who perpetrated some savagery on the lands of their enemies, notably of the Campbells who had earned all that came to them. His kinsman Graham of Claverhouse added lustre to the

[1] And Irish.

Highland name by the immortal and hapless victory of Killiecrankie. Three years had not passed before the Highlands came once more into tragic prominence with the Massacre of Glencoe; and this led naturally to the Risings in 1715 and 1745 against the House of Hanover. It is from 1745, with the break-up of the clan system, the alteration of land tenure, the idea of exploiting the Highlands for money, and (to a large extent, though not wholly, in consequence of that idea) the enormous clearances of men, women and children from the Highlands—it is from 1745 that all these things date.

For over four centuries the Highlands counted in our history: then less than two centuries ago they passed out of the stuff of life to become material for romance, based on a reality which like Prince Charlie had gone and could never return. There is nothing wrong with romance, except that like the statue of Rimmon in Kipling's poem it is a dead god and conceals from its worshippers the fact that the shrine within is empty, or fast becoming so.

The following paragraphs from a letter published in *The Times* last September will illustrate the point. The letter was headed ' ROMANCE ' AND MOIDART.

> The inhabitants of Moidart are practically entirely cut off from the outside world. Their only means of communication with it is by a rough track over the hill or by boat, along a coast open to the full force of the Atlantic gales, upon which they are entirely dependent for all supplies and even for the services of a doctor. If the sea is calm the crofters get their supplies by boat at the rate of 25s. a ton from the nearest station; if the sea is rough, as it usually is in winter, they must carry the goods on their backs for 12 miles or more.
>
> There have been many attempts made to have a road or even a cart track built for these people, but there is never any money available.
>
> They have been promised telephonic communication under the Jubilee scheme, but there is no sign of that promise being fulfilled.
>
> There would always appear to be plenty of money to build trunk roads for the tourists who come north in search of ' romance', but never a penny to help to make life tolerable for the ' natives '.
>
> Romance is a poor substitute for the modern

conveniences—now considered by most to be necessities—of the twentieth century.

The population is, of course, rapidly falling, and unless something is done complete depopulation will result.

The descendants of those who fought with Prince Charles Edward are unable to scrape a living from the land where their forefathers have lived for countless generations.

II

It must be admitted in the first place that this difficult problem is an old one, and secondly that many eminent people have given it their attention—and still it remains. From these premises it might be deduced that the problem is insoluble, and that it is a mere waste of time to trouble about it any more. There are influential men in Scotland who do not wish to hear it mentioned again, and who would be horrified if it were solved along the lines which this book will suggest.

On the other hand, no one except the few who have an interest in keeping the Highlands empty of inhabitants, can doubt that it would be an excellent thing to see them once more the homes of a thriving, strong and happy race: and it would imply a great lack of faith in you and me if we could say that anything so good and so essentially desirable was beyond achievement. In Britain to-day it is unfashionable to talk of faith, in this sense, as having any power at all. The fashionable phrase is 'Money talks'. Even the Socialists have lost their faith; accepting the theory that money talks, they try to get the better of the rich man who holds to his selfish privilege, only by taxing him out of his position.

This is not enough. Where there is no faith or idealism, the people are bound to perish, whoever may possess the money. We must see to it that an *Ideal* shall talk.

I know that the eminent people who do not wish to see this problem solved, are genuinely convinced that it cannot be solved. They point to the number of young men and women leaving the Highlands every year to find jobs in Glasgow or further south, or in the Empire, and they say: ' If there were a future in the Highlands, would these young men and women be leaving their homes and the land they love? How can you stop them leaving, and still more, how can you expect anyone else to go in and take their place? Anyone who invested his capital in such a scheme would end up in the Bankruptcy Court.'

These words are a challenge to the united wit and determination of the people of Scotland. Let it be admitted that if the thing had been easy, it would have been done long ago. Let it be equally admitted, that because we have set our minds to it and are as a nation resolved to see it done, it shall be brought about in the near future.

If our old men (and those who are old in spirit) say it is impossible, they should remember what Hitler has been able to do along these same lines in Germany. He has done it there by force, with the national spirit behind him. In Scotland it must be done in freedom by the nation's will alone, under leadership like that once given by the King of Scots. The problem, though partly political and economic, is more than that. Certain things which on the level of politics and economics alone are genuinely impossible, become possible as soon as you lift them on to that higher plane 'there where', as Dante wrote, ' what is willed can be done.'

III

I wish indeed to emphasise that this ideal which we shall be discussing, will be proved in the later chapters of this book to be realisable. We shall not conjure up a vision in bright and glorious colours, and then be obliged to dismiss it as the product of a dream. None the less, the vision must inspire us along the whole of the road. We should otherwise not know what we were doing nor where we were going, and we should certainly stop before the end for want of courage. The vision therefore must be with us at the outset. When the day comes that we see it realised, then will be the time to rejoice.

The vision is of more than glens and islands peopled again as in the old days with hardy, happy Scots. It is of a united Scotland. Since 1513 Scotland has been a divided, unhappy people. We have drifted along the centuries, uncertain of our destiny. Now the tide carries us faster than ever, and we have no notion what the end will be. We have not even discovered what it is we want, and so each individual has shifted for himself, and the best brains have generally left Scotland to thrive elsewhere. It is an old story that Scotsmen are found in all the chief seats of the Empire. Have we considered how even this divides the nation? The clever ones who prosper abroad, openly despise the disgruntled ones who stay at home and clamour for self-government. The latter say that Joseph in his coat of many colours is selfish, and he replies that his brethren at home are

Nobodies who wish to be Somebodies.   And so it goes on.

Have we ever considered what that Scotland is, to which we all owe our allegiance, however divided we may be in our outward characteristics and pursuits? The first answer is, the earth and the seas of Scotland. The land and its cloak of waters, these are our eternal heritage: these are what we received from our fathers as our own, and these, by God's grace, we shall hand on to our sons as their heritage from all the Scots who have gone before. There is another heritage too—the Scots tradition, embodied for us in deeds of faith, courage and loyalty, which our fathers have achieved throughout our history, and this tradition lives on, somewhat diluted, in us. But the main theme which gave a purpose to all such deeds, and binds them together like a sheaf of corn in memory's harvest, is the very earth of Scotland, upon which (mostly) and for whose sake these deeds were done.

A UNITED SCOTLAND

It is the other, the lesser Scotlands, that divide us and keep us divided. One man loves the Scotland of Knox, his neighbour loves the Scotland of Mary. One looks back with pride to Claverhouse, another to Balfour of Burly. Some are for the Clans, some for the prudent patriotism of Duncan Forbes. The admirer of Rabbie Burns may have no use for Scott: even Wallace is set up as a man of the people against Bruce as the alien adventurer. 'All these things', might Scotland say with old Jacob, 'are against me.' Loyalties so divided and sometimes so petty are no loyalty to the Scotland whom in our deepest hearts we all love.

Our vision therefore must be first of a united people, united in love for their land and in zeal to see that that land shall be put to its proper use, as the home of happy Scotsmen and Scotswomen in the years to come.

It is indeed only within this framework that the solution lies. You will never get money to build roads in Moidart on the bare ground that the people of Moidart died for Prince Charlie years ago. Moidart and Glenelg and Soay will be rescued, not for themselves— their past history or their present grievances— but as part of the greater Scotland which we must leave to our sons.

IV

It would be an inspiring start if enthusiasm for this single dominating purpose could unite all warring creeds in Scotland. Let Roman Catholic and Protestant join together in a new crusade. Above all, let the Kirk and the people of Scotland be united on this issue as they have never been since the days of the Covenant. Let the people feel the hand of the Kirk leading them, as of old in the cause of Scots independence, so now in this new cause of putting Scotsmen to tend and till the fertile straths and islands of Scotland, which for so long have been the precincts of wealthy strangers. It is a matter not to be tolerated in the reign of George VI and his Scottish

Queen that strangers, however rich they may be, should keep the Scots farmer and peasant from enjoying a living upon Scottish soil.

Direct request should be made to all proprietors of any land which is suitable for settlement, and where settlement has hitherto been forbidden in the interests of sport. There need and should be no wanton interference with sporting rights, but it must be understood that these will give way to human rights. If any wealthy proprietor does not, after due request and then after due warning, admit in practice the justice of this claim, the Secretary of State for Scotland must see quickly that the rights of Scotland to be tilled and tended, and the right of a Scot to make his living upon Scottish soil, shall supersede the proprietary sporting rights which date back no farther, at most, than 1745.

To some this suggestion must seem to imply a radical interference with the sanctity of private property ; others would look on it only as correcting an abuse of private property. Certain it is that if matters were brought to that point, public opinion in Scotland—however tenacious of the right of each man to own his own hearth—would overthrow the supposed right of one man (very often an alien) to keep families of Scots from developing in peace and quietness the land of Scotland. And more than one landmark would be swept down in the struggle. We hope very much that the proprietors will gladly accommodate in suitable places in the Highlands and Islands, any Scots who can make good their living there.

We know well that a wave of the wand will not do it, that you have to consider not only the fertility of the soil and the chances of the fishing, but also the mental outlook of the people, their experience as farmers and fishermen, and their adaptability to new surroundings. The money which the rent of a deer forest brings into a district circulates into many poor Highland pockets, and may lift a burden off the parish and the council rates. The law indeed expressly prohibits the Department of Agriculture from converting into crofters' holdings any forest land when the public interest would suffer thereby, and the money which a rich alien is prepared to find for his own and his friends' pleasure may constitute a public interest. There is also the fact that land settlements made in a hurry and on a large scale have seldom proved a success: the people need time to be absorbed into the countryside. Nevertheless, as things are now, we are simply being carried down the stream much faster than we are rowing up it: since 1912 the Department of Agriculture and its predecessors have settled in new or enlarged holdings between 7,000 and 8,000 men, who with their families may have totalled 20,000 people: yet between 1921 and 1931 the country population of Scotland *fell* by more than 66,000. The problem, therefore, has got to be solved along more drastic lines than the authorities have yet found necessary. The authorities are no more than machines to express the people's will. It is for us to say, first, what shall be done, and then to show the astonished officials that we in our own time can do it.

Scotland will be a happier place in the future if in this matter also there is unity— unity between proprietor and tenant, in their determination each and both together to help and develop Scotland to the farthest of their power. It should be remembered (or let the Kirk be at hand to remind us) that whether we call ourselves proprietors or tenants, we are in fact all tenants, and on a short lease even if we rivalled MacLean of Duart, and could spin out our holding to 100 years. Considered in relation to the land of Scotland which has existed for unknown thousands of years, we are trustees for a very brief part of time, but it happens that the present time is a very critical one, for if we do not act quickly, the Highlands will become within two generations almost a total wilderness.

HUMAN LOVE

Put out the light (said Othello) and then put out
  the light:
If I quench thee, thou flaming minister,
I can again thy former light restore,
Should I repent me:—but once put out thy light,
Thou cunning'st pattern of excelling nature,
I know not where is that Promethean heat
That can thy light relume.

Allow the land to go completely out of
cultivation, and by hard labour and long
patience it might be reclaimed by our
descendants. But once allow the Highlanders
to perish out of their ancient homes, and this
world will know them no more. Others
have recounted the glorious additions that
Highlanders have made along every path of
progress and adventure in British history.
It is enough for me, as it will be for many of
you, to remember some one Highland laddie,
or maybe a Highland lass, to whom we owe a
friendship, or a love, that has lightened our
whole existence. Let each of us ponder how
poor in comparison our individual life would

have been without that intimacy that we remember, and we have a measure of the world's loss if the race of the Highlands were to become extinct.

CHAPTER IV

LIFE IN THE HIGHLANDS

' They shall build houses, and inhabit them; and they shall plant vineyards, and eat the fruit of them.'

ISAIAH LXV, 21

ANY DISCUSSION on the Highland problem ought to start with the question, What kind of life do you envisage for the Highlander? The answer must satisfy two conditions. The life must be one that suits the Highlander's character and temperament, and it must be one for which the Highlands themselves are naturally fitted. In the very interesting discussion which took place in the House of Commons on 10th March 1937 on the second Reading of the Caledonian Power Bill, this essential question was hardly considered, and yet a failure to do so must lead in the long run to much unhappiness.

It is well known that Lord Leverhulme tried to help the Highlanders. His monument is a deserted factory in the Lews. He was a highly successful business man: his intentions were excellent: he spent a very large sum in the attempt to start a great new industry in the Islands: and why did it fail? It failed because he did not understand the 'Highland gentleman'. The commercial motive which had oiled the wheels of all his business enterprises hitherto, proved less strong in the men of the Isles than the spirit of independence, and they declined to enter that industrial power-house above whose doors might well (for Highlanders) be inscribed the motto,

> Abandon hope, all ye who enter here.

The situation in Lewis is now extremely bad. Unemployment is widespread, and a correspondent in *The Times* of August last year reported that:

> The independent and manly character of the people is being undermined by a system which

makes unemployment more profitable than work—
as it now generally is to a crofter fisherman. The
crofters of the Isles have hitherto been their own
masters, accustomed to rely upon their native
enterprise and high skill in seamanship; now they
are being induced to seek service with other people,
however humble and unskilled the work may be
[in order to qualify for the dole]. The quality of the
race is not being improved when fishermen are
seeking work as common labourers on the road.

The situation is so bad that outsiders might
be forgiven for thinking that the men of Lewis
were wrong to reject the offers of Lord Leverhulme. But indeed they were right. The
Macfisheries factory would have taken away
their independence as surely as the dole is
doing at present: but the conditions that
have led to their unemployment can be
removed whereas the factory atmosphere,
the industrialisation and commercialisation
of the Isles, could never have been removed,
and would have ruined the Island independence beyond hope of recovery.

I know that in many quarters such a view
must rank as heresy, but the Highlands are not

the Potteries, and what may suit the men of Staffordshire is not necessarily the right medicine for Stornoway. A distinction must be made, according to men's character and tradition. Nevertheless, the rejection of industrial offers, such as Lord Leverhulme's and now that of the British Oxygen Company to establish a carbide factory at Corpach— though in my opinion both offers were rightly rejected, as unsuitable to the character of the Highlands, and likely to have given their development a permanently false direction— makes it the more essential to find and prosecute with all speed their development on right lines, and such as will give permanent happiness to the inhabitants.

In his *Plan for the Highlands* Mr. Quigley, who is an Officer of the Central Electricity Board, makes the following statement on electrical schemes in the Highlands:

' It is necessary that no further water-power schemes in excess of 50 h.p. should be permitted without its approval,[1] and this approval would be contingent on certain conditions inherent in regional planning, agricultural and landscape amenities, social considerations, and so forth, which have not been adequately considered hitherto.

' An important part of the activities under this head would lie in the provision of equipment and the financing of small schemes where small quantities of water-power are available for local needs. There are certain areas in the Highlands where it is physically and economically impossible to distribute electricity from a central source, and so the development of isolated rural communities on any satisfactory scale would be dependent on the utilization of local water-powers. The combined development of small water-power installations with large central distribution systems has been a characteristic of economic progress in Switzerland for a considerable time, and despite the fact that very large hydro-electric schemes have been built during the last few years, there has been little or no interruption in the equipment of small schemes supplying the motive force for local industrial enterprise. It is this form of enterprise which will probably be more valuable to the Highlands than the very large electro-chemical and electro-metallurgical

[1] Referring to a suggested Highland Development Board which Mr. Quigley, in common with the Highland Development League, would like to see in control of all activities bearing on the economic revival and reconstruction of the Highlands.

schemes employing only a small body of labour at a few points of production.'

A householder in one of the inner Islands set up a small dynamo on the mountain stream above his dwelling, and, without the necessity of storing power, supplied himself at very little cost with electricity for cooking, light, central heating and hot bath water. This is an example to be followed.

Many people see in the tourist industry the one hope of saving the Highlands, but they forget the long northern winter. The tourist traffic is an important asset to the Highlands (it has proved a godsend to enterprising crofters) but it is practically confined at present to the three holiday months July, August and September, and those who would like it to become the chief industry there, should ask themselves what those Highlanders do in the winter who make their living out of tourists. A West Coast hotel-keeper writes as follows:

THE TOURIST INDUSTRY

The visitor from the South comes up to enjoy the beauties of our scenery for only three months of the year—July, August and September. For the remaining nine months of the year we Highlanders just exist—that is all. There is practically no work for us during the long winter months, so our young people just drift into Glasgow if they can, while the older folk go to sleep to save light and fire. Scenery or no scenery, anything that brings us work and employment for the nine months visitors from the South are absent is welcome, and I feel that no one can write fairly about the conditions of the Highlands unless he has spent a whole winter with us.[1]

That is right. The Highlanders cannot survive if they are to depend entirely on tourists, and they will not survive in any form worth having if their people are to be chained to the wheels of Big Business, whose psychological effects are intensely corrosive.

This is not to deny the value of the tourist traffic, which indeed should be encouraged and developed on a much larger scale than at present. Here again, however, the atmosphere of big business—the Blackpool touch— is not wanted by any of the Scottish holiday

[1] Letter in *The Times*, 8th March, 1937.

resorts, and least of all in the Highlands. Tobermory does not aspire to be a second Rothesay, and Rothesay has similarly disclaimed any intention of aping Blackpool. Why is this? The fundamental reason is that Scotland, however unwilling she might be to say it in public, knows that there are values greater than cash can offer, and among these is the beauty of the scenery and the independent spirit of the people, both of which would be gone if the profit-motive were ever allowed to reign supreme in Scotland. It did so reign in the early years of the Industrial Revolution, with consequences from which we still suffer very severely to-day.

II

The Problem is, what is to become of the Highlands and the Highlander; the answer must be governed by that which the Highlands and the Highlander have it in them to be. Lord Leverhulme and others have found that the Highlander is not fitted by temperament and disposition to make a good industrial worker.

This is a controversial subject ; arguments were brought forward on both sides when the Caledonian Power Bill was under review, and again in a wireless discussion last April. Flora Macleod of Macleod, who took a prominent part in that discussion, tells me that her Skye friends are never tired of impressing on her that what they want is regular work at a regular wage with the security of insurances and benefits attached. She adds that she has frequent occasion to deplore the lack of enterprise which is content to see vegetables imported from the South rather than grown on the local crofts by private initiative.

The West Highlander is often accused of being lazy. His apparent indifference or idleness may be due partly to the climate but a profounder reason is this, that unless the Highlander is thoroughly interested in what he is doing, he is only a shadow of his true self. It takes a job with adventure and risk

in it to bring out all his marvellous powers of
resolution and endurance.

The numbers and percentages of employees
at the Kinlochleven and Lochaber Works in
July 1937 are as follows:

	Kinlochleven	Lochaber
Number of employees -	622	383
Highland - - -	71% [1]	67%
Lowland - - -	23%	25%
English and Welsh -	3%	4%
Irish - - - -	3%	4%

The number of men employed by the British
Aluminium Company at the Lochaber Factory
is expected to be almost doubled when the
present addition to the factory is completed
in two years' time.

On the question of amenities the Provost of

[1] This figure requires qualification. It includes men whose
families have worked for nearly a hundred years at the slate
quarries of Ballachulish, and men from Fort William and Inverness
whose outlook is distinctively urban. I was informed at Kinlochleven that the ' traditional ' Highlander—whom Southerners know
chiefly as a ghillie—is not as a rule suited to internal factory work.
The ' traditional ' Highlander is of course becoming rarer every
year.

AMENITIES AT FORT WILLIAM

Fort William has been so good as to send me the following statement of his opinion:

> 'The British Aluminium Company have erected a factory on a barren moor which presented no attraction whatsoever to the eye, and the buildings have been so contrived and so laid out that they have rather an attractive appearance, and are a feature in an otherwise featureless tract.'

He continues:

> ' The Company have designed a model village. . . . Every house has its own garden, and the streets will become through time avenues of trees. Tennis Courts and a Bowling Green have been provided, and the Company are at present reclaiming sufficient land to provide a Playing-field. There are, besides all this, miles and miles of glens where both parents and children can enjoy freedom and fresh air at any time they wish.'

Kinlochleven to-day looks like a small town from the English Midlands, and in spite of the magnificent scenery which surrounds it, the inhabitants have naturally become infected by the materialistic ' spirit of the age '. They may keep *ceilidhs*, as the Highland Societies do in Glasgow and London, but they have lost the old outlook of the glens and islands. The truth is that the industrial employees in the Fort William neighbourhood are not real Highlanders. The test is not how near they live to the foot of Ben Nevis, but how near they have come to losing their individuality in that mass-mind which is of all things the most alien to the Highlander. If it had been possible for him both to preserve his native outlook and to adapt himself to factory surroundings, the situation would have been different. But the two things, as might have been expected, are as repugnant to each other as alkali and acid; either he becomes an industrialist and no more a Highlander as at Fort William and Kinlochleven, or he obeys his natural instincts and remains his own master.

To say this is to imply no disparagement of those Highlanders who have preferred a minimum salary of £3 a week, to the long and fruitless struggle of many a crofter's life today. Workers at Kinlochleven can buy a motor-bicycle, their women-folk can wear silk stockings, and they can have a high-class radio set; and besides their week's holiday with pay, they can afford to take an extra week or two off in the summer. Some who come from Balla-chulish, or from the Islands, go home to their crofter families to help at the harvest, thus making the best of both worlds—and good luck to them!

Many Highlanders have of course in the past century been absorbed by industry in Glasgow, but the descendants of such people are not recognisable Highlanders now, and the young people who are leaving the High-lands for Glasgow to-day will likewise lose the ancient pattern of the hills: from the point of view of keeping up the Highland stock, they might just as well have migrated to Australia. They are lost to us.

The first step in the solution of the prob-lem is to *make life worth living for a young Highlander in the Highlands*. He does not want industrial employment, and will never settle down to it so long as he has the hills around him. Let him once drift into Glasgow, with nothing but blank walls and pavements and city minds about him, and he will make shift with a factory job like anyone else and very soon become like anyone else. But his gift from his ancestors was not to be one of a crowd, but to be himself. This is what he can be, and wants to be, in his native hills and Scotland's duty is to provide him with the opportunity.

The staple industry of the Highlands is, and always must be, agriculture—not in the restricted sense of ploughing and a regular rotation of crops, for which many parts of the Highlands are unsuited, but a life derived ultimately from the soil, with its handmaid fishing, which is a life derived from the sea.

These are, and must always be, the two pillars of the Highlands. If the tourist traffic, and rural industries principally designed to cater for tourists, can be built up in further support of Highland life, so much indeed the better. But we are bound to look at first things first, and not to delude ourselves into thinking that some secondary occupation or employment will do equally well. The Highlands must grow to stand largely on their own legs, and this they can only do if they produce enough food not only to supply their own needs, but to build up a substantial export sale to the industrial belt and the big towns.

There is no question that the market is there, large and hungry, at the very door of the Highlands. That is something to build upon. The problem is not one of creating a demand, but of *producing* in a climate and on soil which are not in all respects friendly, and of *marketing*, i.e. of getting the produce transported from widely scattered outposts and sold in the big centres at a price which will pay for the transport and also remunerate the farmer.

Once you have these two problems of production and marketing from the Highlands settled, you have settled the Highland problem. For the young Highlander is not wanting to leave the Highlands if a good life is free to him at home: all the subsidiary difficulties, of housing, roads, education and the other amenities which in some parts are seriously lacking, will settle themselves along natural channels very quickly as soon as it is once established that *a good life is open to the young Highlander in the Highlands*. By a good life he means an independent and satisfying life, based either on the soil of a Highland glen, or on the sea.

This I believe to be the right order of handling the problem—to show first, beyond any dispute, that agriculture in the Highlands *can* be made to pay and to yield a good life for a man and those whom he supports; national feeling in Scotland and the Government together then to show that, this being proved possible in theory, it will be made possible and on a sufficient scale in practice. The disposition to make use of this proved opening certainly exists in Scotland. The discouragement that hangs over individuals in Scotland to-day is largely due to a sense of frustration, which clear leadership showing what *can* be done would remove, as mists are dispelled by the force of the sun. We are not by nature given to despair: we are only befogged, and in a thick fog progress is impossible.

The chapters by Sir John Orr which follow are intended as the first beams to dispel that fog. To become fully effective, they must be followed in their turn by a national determination and Government action along the lines which Sir John Orr marks out.

When the factor of individual growth is thus released to play its natural part once more, when the will has been made free and life has begun to stir again where it has long been dormant, there will be not only an increasing demand for roads, piers, harbours, fertilisers, a higher standard of living and of happiness, but an increasing power and means to supply them. For the most improbable of all things will have happened: the machine of government will itself have come to life.

CHAPTER V

SCOTLAND AS IT IS

BY SIR JOHN ORR

LIKE MOST Scotsmen who have given the
matter any thought, the author of this book
feels that things are not going well with Scotland. Our contribution to the building up of
the British Empire has been out of all proportion to our population, and yet our standard
of living is lower than in England or the
Dominions. We have had such a poor share
in the prosperity of the Empire that it has
been suggested that the whole of Scotland
might well be scheduled as a distressed area.
Many are beginning to feel a grudge against
England on the ground that it takes away both
our money and our ablest sons. In material
prosperity we are largely dependent upon

England and in recent years we have lagged
further and further behind. More and more
London becomes the headquarters of Scottish
business and administration. It has become
the real capital of Scotland, with the result
that our national culture languishes and we
affect an English culture which is ill adapted
to our national traditions and character.

This feeling of discontent with the trend of
Scottish affairs finds expression in the attempt
to form a national party, in the demand for a
Scottish Parliament, in movements for the
preservation of the Doric dialect or of the
Celtic language. Efforts such as these, though
well meant, deal with symbols rather than
with realities. What difference would it make
to the average workman or the dole drawer
whether he speaks English or Doric? No
Celt, whatever sentimental attachment he has
for his clan, and however willing to attend
clan gatherings or a Caledonian Ball in London, is willing to exchange a comfortable living in the South for a low standard of living in

a Highland glen merely for the pleasure of speaking Gaelic instead of English. We are a very sentimental people, but we cannot live on sentiment, nor will our resentment at the greater prosperity of England be of much help in improving matters. The bleating of a national party about grievances against England is as futile as the grumblings of a man with a sore head.

This feeling of uneasiness and discontent with the present state of affairs in Scotland may well be the first step towards a national movement for the re-birth of Scotland. Mr. MacLehose has got beyond this first step. He looks not to the past or even the present, but to the future. In his vision he sees Scotsmen enjoying a fuller, healthier and happier life. He sees people at present living in the slums of our cities living on the land, developing the natural resources of the country. He sees the Highlands being repopulated with a vigorous independent race, retaining the characteristics of Highlanders and enjoying a standard of living as high as the urban population of the South. He thinks that if his fellow-countrymen could see the vision as he sees it, we might have a great national movement to make his dream come true—a movement which would give our nation a purpose and an ideal which would enable it to find its soul and bring back the glory that was Scotland.

If we are going to plan to make Mr. Mac-Lehose's dream come true, we must first be clear about what is wrong with Scotland. What is it we wish to change for the better? There would be difficulty at the present time in reaching agreement on this, because the word ' Scotland ' raises a different conception in the minds of different people. Thus, for example, many wealthy people in London who have rented sporting lands in Scotland, and indeed a number of people who own land, think of Scotland as a place to get a holiday and enjoy sport. If the grouse are plentiful and strong, the rivers well stocked with sal-mon, and the weather good for deer stalking, then there is nothing wrong with Scotland so far as they are concerned. They have no immediate personal interest in the problems of Scotland's industrial belt. In the beginning of August they pass through that belt at night in first-class sleepers with the blinds drawn, to be met in the morning by ghillies and servants, who have already prepared in detail the campaign for the mimic warfare against the grouse, the salmon and the stag. Many of these people live in a world apart; some of them are engrossed with their sport, others with an aesthetic sense and a background of culture, are enjoying the incomparable beauty of mountain, moor and stream. It would be considered a little indelicate in a gathering of these people at a shooting lodge to talk about the sordid conditions of the slums of the South of Scotland, where thousands of the descendants of clansmen who once occupied the Highland glens now lead a sub-human existence.

But could we not build up the new Scotland without troubling these people? After all, they form only a very small proportion of the population. It is true they form less than one per cent. of the population, but their power is out of all proportion to their numbers. In our democratic country money is all-powerful. Indeed, in some ways democracy is the last stronghold of the power of money. These people can hire the means of moulding public opinion through the press, and by other more subtle means. Unless we are going to proceed by a revolution, we must carry these people with us. There is no insuperable reason why this should not be done. The new Scotland can be re-built without abolishing salmon fishing, or grouse shooting, or any other of the sports and pastimes of the wealthy, and without driving out the landlords, provided the wealthy and the landlords will realise that their responsibilities to the State are not discharged when they have paid their Income Tax. The ownership of land should carry the heavy duties and responsibilities which it originally did. A lord was originally a *hláford*, which means literally a loaf guardian. He was responsible for the food supply. He was chosen and given powers over his land so that he might be able to fulfil his duty of providing bread and all else that was necessary to enable his lands to rear and support first-class men. He was more trustee than owner. The retainment of the revenues from the land after getting rid of the duties and burdens of trusteeship which included local Government and responsibility for the welfare of the people on the land, justified the penalizing taxation on land and heavy death duties which brought ruin to the good landlord who was trying to fulfil his duties as well as to the bad who regarded the land as much his private personal possession as if he had created it.

Must we first have land nationalisation before the natural resources of our country can be exploited for the benefit of the people? As a matter of fact, we have already gone far in taking the control of the land out of the hand of landlords. But we must have leaders to rule and direct, and a beneficent landlord who realises his duties and responsibilities and takes a pleasure in carrying them out, is more in accordance with our tradition than a bureaucracy which can be as stupid and tyrannical as a bad landlord. It is not so much a new system we need as the spiritual revival to which Mr. MacLehose refers which will enable us to work the present system better. If it cannot be done without national-isation, then nationalisation must come; but let us see first whether or not the overwhelm-ing majority of landowners are not willing to take their place as the leaders in the movement for the new Scotland. Many of them are first-class men of outstanding ability, who would be the leaders no matter what the system of land tenure was. These men are already carrying out the duties of a landlord, improv-ing their lands in the interests of farmers and farm workers, and doing the work of local government with the respect and goodwill of the whole community. There are a few who still believe in the ' divine right ', and act as if the land and the people on it are there merely to be exploited. These are the kind who would prohibit people keeping poultry on their land for fear the poultry might interfere with the pheasants, and are quite indifferent as to whether the people of Scotland need more eggs, or whether there are families on the land who might make a good living by keeping poultry. Landlords of that type are mostly of the older generation and out of touch with modern social and economic developments. They are survivals from the last century and should be allowed to die out in peace. Let us have a national awakening, and the great majority of landlords will rally to the movement for the new Scotland and be found amongst its leaders.

To another group of people absorbed in money-making the word ' Scotland ' means the industries and trade of Scotland. If trade is doing well, Scotland is doing well. They are interested to see unemployment figures going down, not so much because that means a higher standard of living for the men who were formerly unemployed as because it is an indication that business is good, more money is in circulation and better profits are being made. In the early nineteenth century our ruthless industrial leaders developed our coal fields, our iron and steel industries, our factories, our shipbuilding, and all the trade and business and money-making that arose from these, with a single eye to the making of money. That the common people of Scotland should share in this prosperity was no concern of theirs. They imported work people from Poland and from Ireland, who were accustomed to a very low standard of living and were therefore willing to work for low wages. That ruthless exploitation of the natural resources of Scotland in the selfish interests of a few has left us our legacy of desolation to be found in the industrial belts of Scotland and the embitterment of the submerged working classes in the industrial areas. The gifts of money made to the Church and to charities is poor compensation for the damage done to the Scottish people. If in 1837 there had been a national plan for Scotland, we might have had all the wealth we have to-day with, in addition, a high standard of living for the Scottish people, and the people with wealth of money or of land would have enjoyed in security all the luxuries they have with the respect and goodwill of the people of Scotland. The smouldering discontent of the poorer classes and the more dangerous feeling of indignation among the youth of the better-educated classes, has its origin in the *laissez faire* doctrine of the early nineteenth century, according to which the general community existed to be exploited and the accumulation of wealth carried no responsibility other than occasional donations for religion, learning or charity.

But this worship of money and the

subservience of everything to money-making which reached its peak in the industrial revolution of the nineteenth century, and made that period possibly the most degrading in the whole of the history of our country, has already begun to pass. In England, probably more than in Scotland, industrial leaders have begun to recognise their responsibilities. Many firms now realise that even from the commercial point of view it pays to have well-paid, well-fed and well-housed workpeople. The good employers no longer regard their men as mere ' hands ', but as human beings, and public conscience now demands that the first charge on any industry should be the adequate remuneration of workers.

We need our industrial leaders, and we need a system of competition which will enable the men with the qualities of leadership to rise to the top; but these men must have a wider vision than merely accumulating wealth for themselves. They must realise that our

trade and our industries are national property
to be run for the good of the country as a
whole. This wider objective will not worsen
the position of our industrial leaders. Scotsmen know a good man when they see him.
They find it difficult to be servile: but what
man, except someone with an inferiority complex, wishes servility? Leaders of the type we
need will not only get all the emoluments they
have, but in addition the loyal service and
affection of their work-people.

Then there is a patriotic class far more
numerous than the big landlords or the industrial and commercial magnates, to whom the
word ' Scotland ' is associated with the real
or imaginary glories of the past. These are
the enthusiasts who run the Burns Clubs, the
Caledonian Clubs and Scottish societies for
preserving the Doric or the Gaelic or promoting some other patriotic object. Every real
Scotsman feels a glow of pleasure in the company of these people, who have a homely,
honest enthusiasm and a pride of race which

carries us back to the tales and sentiments of our childhood days. They render invaluable service by keeping the national spirit alive. But there is a danger of the patriotic fervour evaporating in mere sentiment. Harping on the past with no plans for the future is too suggestive of national senile decay. It may become too much like the old man, out of touch with the present, mumbling about the glories of his departed youth.

This patriotic sentiment might be turned to still better account if, instead of being so much absorbed with Burns and the life and literature of the past, it was more concerned with the problems of the present and the future. ' Bruce, Wallace and other Scottish heroes ' is a favourite toast at St. Andrew dinners. These were great heroes, but the fight they fought is past and done with. We should remember them only as an inspiration for the heroes of to-day and to-morrow, who must fight if Scotland is to be made a land worthy of their descendants. Scotland has a great heritage of personal freedom and liberty of thought and speech. It is well that we should recall the leaders of the past and praise these great men and our fathers who begat us, but they should be recalled only as an inspiration for us, their sons, to emulate their great deeds. At Scottish gatherings our eyes should be on the future more than on the past. A suitable toast for Scottish gatherings would be ' The Scotland of 1957 '.

We have spoken on some of the conceptions which the word ' Scotland ' raises in the minds of different people. For our purpose when considering the future of Scotland, we will think in terms of the Scottish Nation which includes all classes, even the unemployed in the slums. Indeed, we must give these special consideration, because if we are going to plan for the improvement of our people, we should concentrate our efforts on where improvement is most needed. We must build the new Scotland from the bottom upwards. We will assume that in national planning the natural resources of the country should be developed in the interest of the people of the country and that industry and trade must have as its ultimate objective the welfare of the people as a whole.

Now when we consider the condition of the people it may be difficult for many people to realise that there is any cause for uneasiness or discontent with the present state of Scotland. The standard of living of the people, even of the poorest, has been rising steadily, and rising faster in the last ten years than in any previous decade. Our people are better housed than they were; our children are better fed than their parents when they were children; the average length of life has been prolonged probably by as much as five or six years in the last decade; and social measures such as unemployment benefit and outdoor relief have taken the worst edge off poverty. There is much, therefore, to support the view that things are going well, and that it is only fanatics and fussy busybodies who talk about the need for a national movement for a new and better Scotland.

But we should compare the present conditions of life in Scotland not with the past, but with what they might be in the future. The conditions in all countries are improving. We might first see whether conditions in Scotland are improving as fast as conditions in other countries. Nearly all European countries have had for a number of years national schemes for raising the standard of living of the poor. Progress is being made more rapidly in some countries than in Scotland. If we compare Scotland not with the best but with its nearest neighbour, we find that, according to the Report of the Department of Health for 1936, the proportion of houses unfit for human habitation in Scotland is six times as great as in England. In Scotland 16·2 per cent. of the work-people are unemployed compared with 9·2 per cent. in England, and the number of people on outdoor relief is proportionately greater. Hence, poverty is worse in Scotland than in England.

This poverty is reflected in both bad housing, to which I have referred, and in bad feeding. The bad housing and the poor feeding is reflected in the health of the people. Probably the best indication we have of the health and vigour of a race is the ability of its women to rear their children. Infant mortality rate in Scotland last year was 82 compared with 57 per thousand in England. Taking all the European countries, Scotland stands fourteenth on the list. The idea held by many people that compared with other races we Scots are a hardy race of outstanding physique is no longer true. At one time we probably were outstanding in physique, and though we have improved, other races have improved so much more rapidly that we are now far down the list. The extent to which England has shot ahead of us in recent years is shown by the fact that although our infant mortality rate is now 50 per cent. higher than in

England, in 1900 it was actually 15 per cent. lower.

There is no need to continue the rather distressing comparison of the standard of living and the health and physique of Scotland with England or Scandinavian countries, where the standard is even higher than it is in England. Let any person walk through the slums of our cities and look at what Mr. Elliot referred to the other day in the House of Commons as 'the heaped up castles of misery', where human beings are huddled together, and consider the kind of life that must be led, under conditions where the income is insufficient to purchase sufficient food to rear healthy children, where three or four families have only one w.c. among them. Let him look at the children there and compare them with the children of the well-to-do. Let him look at the women of between thirty and forty and compare them with women of the same age among the well-to-do. That is the fate of a large proportion of the Highland population which was drained into the cities in the nineteenth century. Under these conditions we find the descendants of clansmen, while the homesteads of their grandfathers in the Highland glens are crumbling to ruins. It is under these conditions that about a third of the children of Scotland are being reared. We cannot regard Scotland as prosperous while these conditions last. This is not the Scotland we wish to hand on to our sons.

CHAPTER VI

SCOTLAND AS IT MIGHT BE

BY SIR JOHN ORR

THE SCOTLAND of the future which Mr. Mac-Lehose sees is a country in which every Scottish family will have a house in which a family can live in decency, and have sufficient of the right kind of food to rear children, so that they will attain their full inherited capacity for health and physical fitness. He wants to reverse the nineteenth century flow of the population from the country to the towns. He wants to see a much larger proportion of our people living in economic freedom, with a high standard of living in our country districts, in the lowlands and in our Highland glens. He wants those who are left in the cities to have the high standard of living he demands for those on the land. If that were done the lives of the poorer half of the population of Scotland would be transformed. Environmental conditions would be such that our inherited capacity for physique would get full scope. We would become a race as vigorous as the Scandinavians. Our infant mortality rate in Glasgow, which is now about 100, would come down to the level of Oslo, where it is below 30. Give us those conditions, and in physical and intellectual vigour no race in the world would surpass us.

Can this be done? Not only can it be done, but if it is not done the present economic system will collapse. The application of science to industry has enabled us to produce real wealth in such abundance that our trade system cannot dispose of it. The so-called glut even of foodstuffs is so great that the Government has had to resort to measures of restriction of production and imports. The way to relieve the congestion and prevent a collapse is not to limit production, but to

increase consumption and raise the standard
of living. We could consume all the present
production of food and far more. To bring
the national diet up to the level recommended
by the Government Advisory Committee on
Nutrition, Mr. George a statistician, estimates that we would ' require an increase of
$33\frac{1}{3}$ per cent. in our dairy herds and the complete elimination of all manufacturing processes '. This means increased production on
the land in this country and increased imports of butter and cheese. In the case of
eggs he says ' we must either increase our
poultry population by 50 per cent. or double
our imports.' We need also a greatly increased consumption of fish and fruit. Our
Scottish farmers are unsurpassed in skill, and
our land could produce all the milk, eggs and
fruit required, and our fishing industry all the
fish required to bring the diet of the poorer
half of the population of Scotland up to the
standard recommended by the Government
Committee.

THE WILL TO DO IT

But in addition to food we need houses. We can get the material to build houses and our workmen have the craftsmanship. The men who build luxury liners like the *Queen Mary* to carry foreigners could surely build decent houses for our Scottish families.

For food and housing, the two primary necessities for rearing a vigorous race, we do not lack resources of either men or material; what we lack is the will to do it. But the will to do it can only come through a great spiritual revival, which will bring about a new assessment of values. It could all be done in one decade if our industrial magnates instead of concentrating their attention entirely on money-making would take a pride in the number of men the industry can support, and boast of the high standard of living enjoyed by the men in their industry; if our land-lords took a pride in the number of people living on their lands and in their standard of living; if they would boast not about the number of salmon and grouse they have killed, but of the health and physique and intellectual vigour of the children in their domains; if our sentimental Scots instead of boasting about the rather mythical glories of the past would direct their patriotic fervour to the improvement of conditions for the future; if those who claim to be the leaders of our Highland clans would regard it as a shame and disgrace to their clan for any member to be living under the sordid conditions of a city slum, while the lands of the clansmen are desolate and empty.

But we cannot hope to do this without a revolution. We have had evolution and the 'process of gradualness' for the last fifty years, a process in which all progress was estimated in terms of money, wage levels, salaries and dividends, and we have still a desolate industrial belt, an empty countryside and the slums with their poverty and misery. We need a revolution which would give us a different index of prosperity. We could get no better index than the standard of living of the poorest.

You cannot raise that without raising the whole structure of society.

We need not be afraid of a revolution. Scotland has had revolutions in the past and been a great deal the better of them. We had a religious and political revolution in the sixteenth century, when the soul of Scotland was shaken to its depths and peers and peasants signed the National Covenant, some of them with their blood. That revolution gave Scotland its religious and political freedom. We had a revolution at the end of the eighteenth century. About 1750 the agriculture of Scotland was more backward than that of any country in Western Europe. The nation then got a new assessment of values. The energy which had been dissipated in religious and political fighting was directed towards the land. Landlords, farmers and peasants and even clergymen worked with enthusiasm in creating a new Scottish agriculture. Within fifty years the old mediaeval system of agriculture which had continued until the eighteenth century was revolutionised, and in the early years of the nineteenth century our methods of agriculture were probably the best in Europe, and English landlords were taking Scottish farm workers south to introduce the Scottish system of agriculture to England. During the Great War the industries of Scotland were reorganised to provide ships, guns, munitions and other war material, and our manhood organised into fighting units. In Scotland we do things thorough. So thorough was the revolution of our industries for the purpose of war, that when the war ceased the bottom fell out of our industries. That is probably the main reason why the post-war depression was so much more acute in Scotland than in England. If a national movement with the enthusiasm and discipline and the organisation of men and material such as we had in the war were brought into being, and directed towards raising the standard of living of the great masses of the people of our country, beginning with the poorest, then within a decade we could have a new Scotland with no slums and none of the misery and degradation of the depressed areas. We might have done this any time in the last fifty years if we had had the will to do it.

Let us assume that Mr. MacLehose's plea will be listened to, and that we will have a revolution; one without bloodshed and without bitterness; one in which we will pull down nothing which should be conserved nor lessen the material prosperity of any class. This can be done, because if we think in terms not of money but of real wealth, we have or can produce in abundance everything we need to raise the standard of living of the poorest without depriving the more fortunate of any of their material possessions.

If we are going to have a revolution to carry out a Scottish national plan, we must have a definite objective. Let us have a modest, simple objective that all classes will understand, and let us set down in our plan only what we know we can accomplish. Let us limit it to food and housing. For food we will set out to get nothing extravagant, no luxuries, merely a diet on the standard which the Government Committee has said is necessary for health. And for housing, a standard which would allow a comfortable house so that not more than two people sleep in a bedroom, and a separate sanitary convenience for every family.

To bring the diet of Scotland up to this level would involve an increased production of from 20 to 50 per cent. of milk, eggs, fruit, vegetables and fish. This means the re-organisation of Scottish agriculture for increased production. This can be fitted in to a policy of increasing the number of people on the land. Scotland must increase its rural population if it is to retain its national character. No nation which has not got a large section of the population rooted on the land is safe.

But even if we had a scheme for establishing more families on the land we would need to find means to induce them to stay there. People left the land in the past because the standard of living was higher in the cities. They trecked down from the poverty of the Highlands in the hope of a higher standard of living in the towns of the south, and the ablest of them trecked further south to seek their fortunes where there was more money to be made. There is more money to be made in buying and selling things than in producing them. There is more money to be made in finance than in ordinary trade. If the people are to be kept on the land this must be reversed. As good a living must be made on the land as in the towns.

But the mechanisation of farming is driving people off the land. More and more is being produced with less and less labour. Another difficulty about the settlement of people on the land is that the best farming land has been taken up by the big farmers. It was too often the inferior land that the small man got, and consequently the old crofts did not pay. The land was generally poor and the economic unit was too small, and consequently the crofter had to accept a standard of living below that of the workman in the town with the result that the family migrated to the town, and the homes of the crofters which reared healthy families though they had to work hard, crumbled to ruins and the fields got merged into larger holdings.

We have schemes for land settlement, but the numbers being put on the land do not compensate for the numbers of crofters and farm servants leaving the land to add to the congestion of the cities. If we wish a larger proportion of our families reared in the country we must have much more ambitious schemes for land settlement. We must experiment along new lines and the nation must be prepared to pay. Fortunately, the additional food we need, *e.g.* milk, eggs, fruit and vegetables, to bring our national diet up to the standard required for health is the kind of produce best suited for small farms. But until the nation has decided to embark on a national scheme for attaining the double objective of producing the additional food needed for health reasons, and of getting a much larger proportion of the population on the land, it is hardly worth while considering new schemes. The following suggestions are merely examples of methods which might be investigated to see if they are worth trying.

We might have large farms fully mechanised with the minimum of continuous labour, and a small village settlement beside the farm, the people in the settlement getting seasonal labour, e.g. a large farm with five or six whole-time workers, engineers rather than farm servants, and about forty or fifty other people getting three to four months' work on the farm during the year, and the rest of the time working in their own small holdings on which they produce the most of their own foodstuffs and have a surplus of eggs, tomatoes, honey and handicraft material, which might be marketed through the large farm organisation.

These settlements might provide a reservoir of labour for our industries. When labour in the towns was scarce some of the men might move into the towns. Facilities for travel are now so good that some might work in the towns and live in these villages. In times of depression and unemployment these men would be living in healthy surroundings with something to do and an interest in life instead of living huddled together in the slums of the cities.

If small independent units are to be made to yield a standard of living high enough to induce people to stay on them, then they would need to get their raw material, feeding stuffs, manures, etc., at the same price as the large units, and they might need to get a better price for their produce than the large units. The Marketing Boards might be organised to do this. For example, they might give x pence per dozen for, say, the first 500 dozen eggs, $x - \frac{1}{2}$d. for the second 500, and $x - $ 1d. for all in excess. This would bias the system in favour of the small farm but still allow scope for enterprise and initiative on the part of the big farmer with organising ability and plenty of capital. It may be worth while having a scheme on these or other lines which will favour the small farmer. In these days, when industry and business run to big combines, with everyone employees and servants, except the board of directors, there is a danger of the national characteristics of virile independence and initiative being lost. To preserve these it may be worth while taking steps to prevent the small independent men, shop-keepers, traders, farmers, from being crushed out.

If it were desired to create an agricultural population in the more fertile parts of the Highlands, we would need to consider what branches of agriculture were best suited for these districts. The Orkney Islands have shown what can be done with poultry. Another branch which might be developed is the production of store cattle. Stapledon's work in Wales has shown that the productivity of the grassy hills can be greatly increased. In the milder climates of the Western Highlands there is a luscious growth in summer. Some of this might be preserved in small silos for winter feed, and so increase the number of stock which can be kept. The higher subsidy being paid by the Meat Commission for home-produced animals should favour the production of store cattle in the Highlands, and might form the basis of a national scheme for increasing the number of cattle which in turn would help to tramp down the bracken that is now covering land which at one time supported families.

If agriculture is to be made profitable in the Highlands, then the Marketing Boards would need to bear the cost of transport. If in some of the Highland glens they could get their feeding stuffs, manure and other material at the same price as on the outskirts of the great consuming centres, and get the same price for their produce, it might be possible to make agriculture profitable in these outlying districts. But this would involve more labour to produce food for Scotland, and the nation would need to decide whether or not the repopulation of the Highlands and other outlying parts of Scotland is worth the extra labour.

It is not worth while considering putting factories in the Highlands. If you wish to make the Highlanders factory workers it would be cheaper to bring the Highlanders down to the factories. The only kind of factories which are worth while considering for the Highlands are possibly fish-canning and fish-curing, and small factories for the canning of fruit and vegetables, provided it is established that there is sufficient fertile land to grow enough to warrant factories.

The problem of provision of food and the settlement of people on the land should be considered in relation to the problem of housing. The housing scheme would need to be taken for Scotland as a whole in the light of the agricultural development and redistribution of the population. The number of brick-layers and masons in Scotland are quite in-sufficient to build the houses we need quick enough. Why should we not mobilise all the unemployed youths between 16 and 20 who are at present deteriorating physically and morally because they have never been under the discipline of work? These would be set to work helping to build new houses in the towns and new homesteads in the country, improving means of transport and communi-cation in the Highlands and on land reclama-tion. But the amenities of the country must also be increased. Is there any reason why these unemployed youths should not be set to laying out tennis courts and golf courses, not merely for summer visitors, but for the use of the inhabitants?

The mere bringing of these unemployed youths together and giving them something to do would remove the worst evil of unem-ployment, viz. the physical and moral deteri-oration of young Scotland. The youths would be well fed and looked after. Their health and physique would be improved; the work would be an education and a discipline. They would find a meaning and a purpose in life, and no longer have the feeling that they were unwanted and unneeded members of the community. They would be working for their country. The youths themselves would be much happier. Germany has organised its youths into labour camps in a great national preparation for war if war should come. Surely Scotland can organise its youths for these works of national importance which would increase the real wealth of the country and prove valuable national assets. Germany's national drive was done by the enthusiasm of youth. Scotland's youth dawdle at the street corners, and with the exception of some semi-charitable organisations which only reach a few, they are left to their own resources as if Scotland had no need of her youth.

A national scheme for ensuring that every Scottish family shall have a house which will enable them to live in decency, and every Scottish child sufficient of the foodstuffs of special health value such as milk, eggs, fruit and vegetables to enable them to grow up to be a virile race of to-morrow, could be carried out. We have the resources, but the brutal truth is that the general mass of people in Scotland do not want such a scheme. The majority of the well-to-do people, who have the leadership and the organising ability, are not really interested in these things, because they do not see how they would yield a payment to them in money. And the submerged third of the population, living under the conditions they are in and fed as they are, have not the energy to put up a fight for themselves. The future of Scotland is of little interest to people living in the misery of the slums.

An attempt to carry through a national scheme of reorganisation would be resisted by powerful vested interests. Would the house-building trade unions be willing to allow the monopoly of their trades to be broken by a housing campaign carried on by those who are at present unemployed? Would contractors look with favour upon work being done in which they had no chance of making a profit? Even the architects would be loath to see new housing schemes in which they had no hope of any commission. All the different vested interests which are apt to be short-sighted would be liable to oppose any scheme which they thought was going to interfere with their profit-making.

Until we get the spiritual revival which Mr. MacLehose would like to see there is not much hope from the Government. In a democratic country the Government can only carry out the wishes of the people. In this country the people who have the power and influence think mainly in terms of money making and profit, and the Government must do the same. Apart from war, the balancing of the budget, imports and exports and other trade considerations must be the primary interests of the Government of a country of traders. The third of the population consisting of unemployed and poorly paid workmen, whose standard of living is far below what the present material wealth of the country warrants, cause a certain amount of uneasiness. The well-to-do don't like to think of them, for we are a kindly people. We soothe our consciences by charitable organisations and the poor are kept from rising and asserting themselves by periodically giving them a little more. A little extra on the 'dole', a few more houses, a third of a pint of milk at half-price to prevent gross malnutrition among children, and other such social measures take the edge off the bitterness of poverty, and help to keep the masses quiet. Our labour leaders think they have achieved something worth while when they have got these crumbs, when the people they represent might secure their full share of the loaf, which is big enough to supply sufficient for everybody.

THE MONETARY SYSTEM

Scotland is ripe for a spiritual revolution which would enable us to put first things first. A great national scheme for raising the standard of living up to the level which our wealth can support would lead to a revival of agriculture, re-population of the land, a great boom of industry and internal trade, and plenty of room for profit-making. It could be arranged to bring about a period of prosperity for everybody.

Some will ask where is the money to come from. But if the people of Scotland wish a higher standard of living, and the material resources are there and the people are willing to work for it, and the whole scheme is held up because there is no money, then it is obvious that the present monetary system has broken down and no one can expect the country to be run in the interest of an obsolete monetary system. The argument of there being no money is highly dangerous for the people who have money. It may lead to a condition of affairs when their money, which after all is only vouchers, may become of no value. As a matter of fact, in my opinion there is plenty of money in the country if it were used and made to circulate fast enough. The people who have money, and who would need to pay, need not fear, because if it is put in circulation it is all likely to come back eventually into their hands again.

What we want is not more money, but leaders. Will our dukes, our lords and our Highland chieftains come forward to build the new Scotland? They would be more than welcome, and several of them have shown that in such a work they would gladly play their part. What a vision it would bring to the people in the slums and in the depressed industrial areas if they were told that a great national scheme for bringing prosperity to every family in Scotland was being initiated and led by people of that kind. Could we not have a national movement in which these and the equally important trade union leaders and the great captains of industry could combine in a scheme which would win the enthusiastic allegiance of the youths who, dissatisfied with the present state of affairs, join the Communists or the Fascists or some other political group which holds out the hope of rebuilding society on a better basis? Is Scotland, which led the world in the fight for religious and political freedom, which gave civilisation the steam engine, which was the origin of the wealth that the factories of the world produce, now so bankrupt of ideas that it must turn to Russia and Germany for leadership? These systems have an idealism which appeals to youth, because they call for action to do something. And let us make no mistake: great things are being done in these countries. But these systems are not suitable for Scotland, where individual freedom of thought and speech won for us by our forefathers is dearer than material prosperity.

The social and economic structure of society which grew out of the industrial revolution is either collapsing in chaos and disorder or, as in most of the smaller democratic countries, being rapidly adjusted to suit the new age of plenty. The best service which Scotland could render a distracted world would be to show that it is possible to get the co-operation of all classes in an organised national movement to apply the almost inconceivable wealth which modern science can produce to build up a state in which the poorest can lead a full life. If that can be done anywhere without bloodshed and bitterness it can be done in Scotland, where the different classes are of the same blood and understand each other. We have all the same pride of race. The wealthy families of to-day are descended from the working class families of yesterday. Men with Highland names, however poor in wealth, boast—and that truly—that they have the blood of chieftains in their veins. Peer and peasant have stood shoulder to shoulder in many a hard-fought fight in the past. The time has come to close the ranks of all classes for the greatest struggle of all, to lift our Scottish race out of the morass of poverty and confusion which the false ideals of the industrial revolution created.

It is here that the example of our past heroes of Scottish history can help us. Inspired by them, Scotland shook off the domination first of foreign kings, then of her own barons, and finally of the rich monastic institutions which were taking too much from her and giving too little in return. If our forefathers could do that, we can shake off the vested interests in our time, and so make the Scotland of 1957 a happier place for our sons to live in. We have the men, we have the materials, we have the land: all we need is a touch of the ancient fire in our hearts. It may well be that Mr. MacLehose's book will kindle the first glow in the hearts of patriotic Scotsmen.

CHAPTER VII

FISHING AND FORESTRY

' The problem as I see it is this: how to manage efficiently the economic machine and at the same time retain the maximum amount of individual freedom. The Scottish system of family-owned boats represents perhaps the only great industry left in the world to-day where some attempt at solving the problem continues to be made.'

NEIL M. GUNN

A LEADING Scotsman, well acquainted with the Highlands, told me this summer that in his opinion the only hope for the Highlands lay in forestry and fishing. Forestry in Scotland is being very well managed by the Forestry Commission ; the work is of national importance economically, it is being planned as part of a long-term policy approved by Parliament, its area of operation is being continuously extended, and apart from the good which it does to the land itself, afforestation is reckoned to give employment already to at least five men as against every shepherd previously engaged on the grazings planted. One Highland shepherd on an average (the exact figure varies from district to district) covers a thousand acres : for every 200 acres planted, the Forestry Commission settles one man and his family in a croft, i.e. a house with a few acres round about, on which he can keep a cow and some hens—not enough ground to distract him from his forestry, which is a whole-time occupation. It is true of course, that if the Commission were to buy a property at present entirely under sheep, not the whole of the area would probably be suitable for planting : the higher ground, with some rights of winter grazing in the valley, would still be given over to the sheep.

The number of men in direct employment of the Forestry Commission in Scotland last May was 1,645, last January 1,240.

Employment is provided in addition by
the building of houses and steadings for
forest-holders, by the putting up of long
stretches of fences, and indirectly through
the necessary implements and tools which are
usually bought in Scotland. The real advance
in employment will come, and is already
beginning, when the figures quoted above
will be doubled by work in thinning and
felling the crops. Later, when the larger
Forests come into full bearing, mills will be
established permanently and small villages
and homesteads will spring up around them
as in Les Landes in France and all over
Germany.

The Forestry Commission in Scotland (September 1936) had acquired 88 Estates, with
an area of 211,000 acres suitable for afforestation; the actual area of these properties
including agricultural land and unplantable
hinterlands was 449,000 acres. Upon these
properties 334 Forest workers' holdings had
been formed for which about 2,000 acres of

agricultural and pastoral land was assigned. The Estates included areas devastated for war supplies; deer forests, from some of which deer have been cleared; sheep grazings; woodlands and plantations which might have been felled but for the security afforded by State ownership, and of course subjects capable of cultivation, which are either occupied by farmers or earmarked for workers' holdings. In addition to these holdings the Commission has 260 small agricultural lettings under £20 a year, 173 occupied cottages and they have provided 59 Foresters' dwellings. The nurseries required for the provision of forest plants occupy 400 acres and the average labour cost in these nurseries must be about £60 an acre per annum. The programme for Scotland, as in England, is limited by the

(*a*) Government Grant.

(*b*) Acquisitions of land.

(*c*) Advisability of going cautiously in all new schemes.

The Commission has never introduced compulsory acquisition, which would be costly, but has quietly carried out negotiations with owners and agents and this method has so far proved satisfactory.

Suitable properties are of course not always easy to obtain and the Commission should be warmly congratulated on the work they are doing, which is very valuable to Scotland so far as it goes.

That it can never, at the rate of one family to 200 acres, go far enough to re-people the Highlands to any adequate extent, shows that for a true solution of the problem we must look elsewhere. The contribution which afforestation makes and will increasingly make is by no means to be despised, but the two main buttresses of Highland life must still, as in the past, be fishing and agriculture. But in order to face modern conditions, they need taking in hand, or they would decline almost into nothing. Where the soil is poor, as often on the West Coast, fishing has been needed for generations as a make-weight to balance the family budget; it is the decline of the fishing that has driven countless crofters off their holdings, in Skye and elsewhere.

The new standards of comfort to which the British people have grown accustomed, cannot be stopped at Stirling. They must invade the Highlands, or the Highlanders will go south to seek them. The problem of Highland repopulation is therefore to equip Highland agriculture and fishing with means to support a modern standard of life, without subjecting them to modernist industrialisation. Traditionally, Scotland is the country of the small independent man : England is not, and under present conditions most of the odds favour the monopoly-capitalists. The conditions must therefore be altered. Sir John Orr has suggested how to even the odds for Highland agriculture: the same has to be done for the Highland fisherman, whose plight is little understood even in Edinburgh the capital city.

It is a human problem. It is a problem in terms of living individuals, or of individuals who *were* living on the West Coast thirty, twenty, ten years ago and have gone now, leaving their homes deserted. When one thinks of that, one is reminded of Housman's poem:

> The lads in their hundreds to Ludlow come in for the fair,

as they came in from the fishing on the Argyllshire coast not many years back; and he goes on to picture the lads whom, if he returned to Ludlow a summer or two later, he would not see at the fair any more. Those were the ones who should ' carry back bright to the coiner the mintage of man ', who should ' die in their glory and never be old '.

But the fishermen who have been leaving the West Coast in the last thirty years have not been such fortunate fellows. They have died, if they have died yet, not in their glory, but in desuetude—driven out, to a large extent, by the trawlers from Fleetwood in Lancashire that have chiefly contributed to ruining the inshore fishing upon which these men depended for their homes and happiness.

A boatman (aged 38) of Lochgair, a small village on Loch Fyne, told me last summer that thirty years ago there were 50 boys and girls at school with him at Lochgair. A few years later, the number had dwindled to 36. Now the school is shut up. ' Why? ' ' The people are all gone: the fishing is gone.' He told me that in some winters he used to get work on one of the few small boats that still tried to make the fishing pay, but this had been given up, for the fish had become so scarce that there was no profit in sending a boat out. Fish caught elsewhere were sold as ' Loch Fyne kippers ', for the value of the name, but there were practically no herring caught in Loch Fyne now. He was positive, as are all the boatmen both on the West and East Coast of Scotland, that the scarcity of

fish is due mainly to the trawlers and to
seine net fishing.[1]   To re-start the inshore
fishing, and bring it up to its former level of
prosperity, would of course be a huge task:
the mere banning of trawlers from these
waters would not suffice without other positive measures which will be outlined at the
end of this chapter.

No such remedies would in the least avail,
for psychological if not for piscine reasons, to
restore the inshore fishing unless the trawlers
are banned from the Minch for an experimental period of several years.   The Minch
is the channel between the Outer Hebrides
and the mainland or the Inner Hebrides.   By
international law, 20 of these miles are outside the territorial limit of 3 miles from the
coast, a limit based upon the maximum range
of cannon about 150 years ago.   The three-
mile limit was also adopted for fishery pur-

---

[1] The seine net is a net with jaws which close gradually as the net
is hauled up with its catch.   It is used for taking white fish.   Like
the trawl, it inevitably captures many immature fish and the inshore fishing grounds are being in consequence depleted.

poses by Britain, Germany, Denmark, Holland, Belgium and France at the North Sea Convention of 1882, at which time trawling by steam vessels had hardly begun. The Norwegians who alone in Europe possess a coast resembling that of West Scotland, refused to adhere to the Convention on the grounds that the limit proposed was inadequate and incompatible with their interests. They claimed then and claim now a fishery limit four miles outside the outermost line[1] of rocks and islands that fringe their coasts in the same way that the Outer isles fringe ours.

There is therefore an excellent international precedent for closing the Minch to foreign trawlers, and since the North Sea Convention can be voluntarily terminated by any signatory (Article XXXIX), we are not prevented from so doing. There would be nothing in the least immoral or discreditable if we did it.

[1] Thus taking under protection the whole Vestfjord between the Lofoten Islands and the Mainland.

But, we are told, we should suffer retaliation by other countries. What countries? Obviously not Norway. Norwegian vessels in any case do not trawl in the Minch, neither do French and German ones at the present time, but even if they did, France and Germany are not in a position to retaliate against Scottish fishermen, who do not fish in or near French or German waters.

Although very few, if any, foreign vessels trawl in the Minch, there are two foreign countries which would be indirectly affected by its closure. A proposal to close the Minch to trawlers would necessarily involve a similar closure of the Moray Firth, whose inshore fishing is likewise being destroyed by the inroads of trawlers—foreign ones in this case, for Scottish and English trawlers are prohibited from fishing in the Firth. The Scottish Fishery Board Report for 1934 gives the numbers of foreign trawlers observed at work in the Moray Firth since 1907. These figures are very instructive. No Scandinavian trawlers have been seen fishing in the Moray Firth since 1914. At least 90% of the foreign trawlers that have fished in the Moray Firth since the War have been Dutch and Belgian. Is it then for fear of retaliation by these two countries, whose independence we are pledged to maintain against attack—is it for fear of offending them that we dare not close to their trawlers the Moray Firth, which a Scots judge in 1906 declared to lie ' between the jaws of Scotland '?

There are no other countries whose interests are involved,[1] except for the few French vessels which, with Dutch and Belgian, are the only foreign trawlers observed since 1925 in the Firth of Clyde. Together with the Minch and the Moray Firth, it would probably be decided—chiefly for reasons of logic

---

[1] Denmark would like of course to exclude our trawlers from waters near the coasts of Iceland and Greenland. This would severely limit our food-supply and put up the price of fish. But, as we have seen, the Danes do not trawl in the Minch or the Moray Firth, and the closure of those waters would give them no pretext for a general expansion of the 3-mile limit.

which the French would well understand—
to close the Firth of Clyde to trawlers. But
the Firth of Clyde, though it yields a good
supply of herring in normal years, is not a
first-class trawling ground; the number of
French trawlers observed there since the
passing of the Trawling in Prohibited Areas
Prevention Act, 1909, is as follows:

Year 20th Oct.—19th Oct.	No. of French Trawlers	No. of Occasions observed in the Firth of Clyde
Until 1926	—	—
1926-27	1	1
1927-28	6	19
1928-29	2	9
1929-30	3	12
1930-31	—	—
1931-32	3	4
1932-33	15	64
1933-34	18	71
1934-35	16	49
1935-36	14	38

In truth, this talk of ' retaliation ' is so
much camouflage. It is passed on from mouth
to mouth by people who sincerely believe it
to be true, but who are ignorant of the facts.

TRAWLERS IN THE MINCH

What is the real reason why the Minch and the Moray Firth cannot be closed to trawlers?

For an answer there is no need to look far. You need only look at the registration numbers on the ships that actually trawl in the Minch. The numbers are not hidden—cannot be hidden: they are as plain as the number-plate on a car. The vast majority are of English trawlers from Fleetwood. It is very seldom indeed that one sees at Lewis or Lochboisdale or Barra a trawler with an Aberdeen or Granton number: the great majority of East coast men who come to the Minch come after the herring, which is not affected by any proposal to close the Minch to trawlers: in fact, some of the East coast drifters follow the line fishing in the Minch in the winter and their interests are identical with the West Coast fishermen's. It is therefore untrue to say that Scottish fishermen as a whole desire to see the Minch kept open. It is the English trawling interests that desire this.

The Scots are a kindly race, and we should not object to sharing our waters with men from Lancashire if it were possible for our own folk to make a living from the inshore fishing at the same time. But it is not possible. What was once a prosperous white-fish industry has been ruined in the forty years of the trawlers' invasion:[1] only during the war when the trawlers were away, did it revive. *The trawlers must go*.

Trawling, it should be remembered, is done in these six areas:

(a) The West of Scotland.

(b) The North Sea; for a long time the most important area, but now considerably depleted.

(c) Around the Faroes.

(d) Off North Norway.

(e) Off Iceland.

(f) Around Bear Island, and in the Barents Sea.

[1] As early as 1902 trawling was injuring the interests of the Hebridean fishermen (Goodrich Freer, *The Outer Isles*, p. 356).

THE MORAY FIRTH

Compared to the last three areas, the Minch is not very important; the modern trawler, which is equipped for deep sea fishing and to make journeys almost as far as Spitzbergen, is not likely to lose much if told to leave the Minch alone.

In 1907 the Government decided for international reasons not to enforce the prohibition against foreign trawlers in the Moray Firth. The Scottish Fishery Board had issued a bye-law closing the Firth to all trawlers, and a test case occurred in 1906. A foreign skipper (instigated, it is thought, by British trawling interests) was caught trawling in the Moray Firth. He was sentenced, and his appeal to the High Court of Justiciary in Edinburgh was dismissed, one judge remarking that the offence had taken place ' intra fauces terrae ' (anyone who knows a little Latin and looks at the map will agree that the judge was right). Lord Kyllachy, his colleague, repudiated the view that in International Law any part of the Moray Firth could be considered part of the open sea. The Court decided the closure of the Firth to be valid and applicable to all comers. Had this decision been upheld, the inshore fisheries of Scotland would have been in a very much more flourishing state to-day.

It was not to be. The Government reversed the verdict of the Court of Session, set aside the Fishery Board's bye-law by which the Moray Firth had been closed to trawlers, set aside also a bye-law under the same Act closing the Firth of Clyde, and never enforced the provisions of the Sea Fisheries Regulation Act (Scotland) of 1895 for the creation of a 13-mile limit in Scottish waters. That these decisions, through which the Scottish inshore fishings have been virtually ruined, were taken at the instance of English trawling interests is very probable.

The 'international reasons' which determined the Government's decision were:

(*a*) If Britain allowed any exceptions to the 3-mile fishing limit, other countries might begin to make similar exceptions in their own waters, and our trawling interests would suffer.

(*b*) If the 3-mile fishing limit were jeopardised, the 3-mile territorial limit might be questioned too. This was, and remains, an important strategical consideration: the British Navy, for example, would have had a much more difficult task in the War if its right to search vessels on the high seas had been exercisable only outside a distance of say 13 miles, and not 3 miles, from a neutral country's coast.

One may sympathise with the Government in their anxiety to let some sleeping dogs lie, but in the meantime Scottish fishing, one of Scotland's most vital interests, is going from bad to worse,[1] and the Government's inaction is deplorable. It may seriously be questioned

[1] The percentage of unemployed among the adult insured workers at Stornoway in April 1937 was 65.9, an increase of 6.4 on the figure for April 1936. Buckie, another famous fishing port, had 58.5% unemployed out of an insured population of 3,280.

whether the closure of the Moray Firth to foreign as to British trawlers, and the closure of the Minch to all trawlers, would have the troublesome consequences suggested above, for these waters are distinctively Scottish and no fair person can deny it. Because under 300 years of Westminster rule we have not claimed what is our own, that does not mean that we cannot claim it now. On the other hand, if considerations of public policy are the real reason why Scotland's fishing interests must be sacrificed in this particularly galling way—the unemployed fishermen of Buckie have to watch foreign trawlers lapping up fish in full view of Buckie harbour—then Scotland's fishing interests ought to be given some other and sufficient help instead.

Many North-east and East coast fishermen of Scotland are heavily in debt. Their boats are family-owned, whereas the English fishermen are the paid employees of a company. This means that when times are bad, the

English fishermen can have reserves behind them, and the Scottish fishermen have nothing behind them, except a Government which is believed—rightly or wrongly—to favour the English system. It does not mean that, man for man, or boat for boat, the English can do the job better than the Scots. It is Scotland's whole tradition that a man and his family should stand on their own feet and live their own lives as free men without being dictated to by monied interests, and that tradition is worth an effort to save. The people who sit in high places complain that Scotland will do nothing for herself: here all along her coasts are men who have it in their blood to depend only on themselves, who are anxious to win their own livelihood and be a prop to their families as their fathers were—and what do they see? They see the authorities apparently weighting the scales in favour of the foreigner and in favour of English company-owned boats (the latest loan-offers of the Herring Industry Board are suited only to companies,

and are no good to the Scottish fishermen[1]).
For every hundred herring consumed in this
country in 1913, it has been estimated that
only fifty-five are eaten to-day. No one wishes
to deny this and the other difficulties of the
situation; but after the Board's latest Report,
it must be plain that the Scottish fishing fleet
will not be saved at all until the people of
Scotland look upon it as *their* pride and their
responsibility.

Conditions are somewhat easier at Arbroath, and it is interesting to observe the
progress in boat equipment that has taken
place there. Between forty and fifty years ago
all the boats were undecked. The first improvement was a boat half decked, the next

[1] The first suggestion for ' material improvement ' made by the
Herring Industry Board in their Report for the year ending 31st
March 1937 is ' that the vessels and their gear be put into and
maintained in a more efficient condition ' (Para. 48). A Scheme
for advances to owners of drifters for the reconditioning of their
vessels was announced early in March 1936. ' The advantage taken
of this scheme was very small' (Para. 107), and later a new Scheme
was launched, under which the amount to be advanced per vessel
was increased from £375 to £400. No application had been received
by 31st March 1937.

was fully decked but without cabin. Gradually the boats have been improved until the present time when they are fitted out with cabin and motor engine. The latest kind of boat is called a nabbie and is capable of riding through any storm. Formerly the fishermen had two boats, one for herring fishing and a smaller one for white fishing. The present boats are adaptable for both purposes. The number of motor boats engaged in the fishing from Arbroath is now 26.

Until about thirty-five years ago during the months of July and August considerable catches of herring were brought into Arbroath. The herring have practically disappeared off this coast except during the months of January, February and March when they frequent the Firth of Forth and the Firth of Tay. Most of the Arbroath fishermen fish for herring during these months. During the rest of the year they prosecute the white fishing either with lines or seine net. Boats up to 50 feet in length are now allowed to go into the Bays and elsewhere within three miles of the coast and use the seine net for catching plaice of which good catches are usually obtained.

The Provost of Arbroath, Sir William Chapel, who has taken a keen interest in the welfare of the east coast fishermen, writes to me as follows:

It would be of great advantage to the fishermen if the three mile limit was greatly extended. Our fishermen used to get good catches in the vicinity of the Bell Rock about 12 miles distant. Now they proceed to sea to a distance of 30 or 40 miles. If a Trawler happens to see our boats getting good catches off a certain position it swoops down on them and clears up the bank in a day or two. Such a proceeding destroys the position found by our men and deprives them of perhaps two or three weeks' fishing, and they have to search for new fishing ground.

It is generally agreed that unless the Scottish fishermen can learn to co-operate, their days are numbered. The fishermen of Arbroath have in this matter set an excellent example. Independent as they have always been and proud to own their boats, they founded some years ago an Association under the Friendly Societies Act. Nearly all the Arbroath fishermen are shareholders in this Association, whose manager sells the fish by public auction and generally looks after the fishermen's affairs. In consequence they get their oil, lines, ropes and all other gear at very moderate prices, any profit coming back to them in the way of dividends. The Association has proved a great help and is apparently the only one of its kind in Scotland. To combine the principle of private ownership with the great practical advantages of co-operation, so that risks, losses and windfalls shall all to some extent be shared in common, appears to offer the best hope for the East Coast fishermen.

The lives of little men are dictated by great forces, and there is another reason besides international policy why the Minch and the Moray Firth cannot be closed. The British

Trawling interests are anxious to make an inroad on the traditional Norwegian fishery limits, especially in North Norway (Nordland, Troms, Finnmark). At present we have agreed to respect their claims, but a constant propaganda goes on in favour of forcing Norway to adopt the 3-mile limit. If we however were to close the Minch and the Moray Firth, acting according to Norwegian principles of fishery protection, we would be unable to bring any pressure to bear on the Norwegian Government to reduce their limits.

The Norwegian fishermen, not being industrialised like the majority of English fishermen, do not go in for trawling, which demands big capital. The interests of the Norwegian fishermen are identical with those of the Scottish inshoremen. They would like to see the Scots win. They themselves are faced with the same menace, but they have the advantage of an independent government that is ready and able to defend their interests as far as possible. But if the trawling interests win, and Norway is compelled to abandon her 4-mile comprehensive limit and take to trawling herself, industrialising her fishing industry (perhaps with British capital) it will probably mean the extinction of the small independent producer everywhere. An additional trawling fleet manned by Norwegian sailors is not likely to be beaten by that of any other country. The result must be a glut and the forcing of all small fishermen out of business.

For Scotland this would mean a West Coast for ever deserted—no laughter but the cackle of the gulls, no home but the burrows of rabbits.

On a high mountain in the Isle of Mull—a place with a wide view over glen and foreshore, mountains and the blue expanse of waters once alive with boats as the glens had been with homes and hearths—there came to my mind the prayer which is said in Parliament before each day's deliberations are begun:

*O Lord our heavenly Father . . . who dost from
thy throne behold all the dwellers upon earth.*

Of the manhood and womanhood once to
view on this West coast, little is left to-day.
But it may be enough to form the nucleus of a
return, if the appropriate measures are taken.

What finally are those measures?

The closing of the Minch to trawlers would
not be a complete solution in itself, but it is a
necessary prelude to such a solution. So long
as the trawlers are there, catching in great
quantities the cod, ling and haddock which
are the inshore fishermen's chief source of
livelihood, you will get no confidence,[1] and
no capital to refloat the industry.

It must however be said that the harm done
by trawlers is often exaggerated. The spawn
of all our common marine foodfishes (except

[1] Two separate reports, both from experienced men well able
to judge, have reached me this summer from the Island of Tiree.
Both say that the fishing there has been ruined by the trawlers, but
whereas one account is that the trawlers have destroyed the fish,
the other is that the trawlers are made by the Islanders an excuse
for sticking to their crofts and not putting out to sea.

the herring) is in the form of tiny separate eggs which float free in the waters near the surface of the sea. This spawn, unlike the spawn of herring and of marine worms, which is deposited on the sea bottom, is not liable to be injured by the heavy ' ground rope ' of the trawl as it scrapes along the bottom. The trawlers of course sweep up many immature fish and, although the total numbers of cod and haddock which they pull out of the Minch must at any period be small in relation to the total numbers in the Minch, yet this is little consolation to the West Coast fisherfolk. Even though the trawlers do not do such extensive damage as is sometimes said, no one denies that their incursion has made the fishing more difficult for the local people.

The trawlers admittedly do great injury to the herring spawn, which lies on the sea bottom. The recent scarcity of herring on the West Coast cannot therefore be ascribed entirely to the natural vagaries of the herring population—in itself a problem of great complexity, which will need decades of work by highly skilled and highly trained investigators.

But because the problem cannot be completely solved at once, that is no reason why the first steps should not be taken now. These are:

(1) To ban trawlers from the Minch and the Moray Firth.

(2) To establish a West Coast Fishing District, on the lines of those successfully at work in England and Wales.[1] Fishery District Committees are financed out of the general rate; they have the power to make bye-laws regulating the local fisheries, appoint (honorary) officers and paid officials, and inflict fines, etc.

The South Wales Sea Fishery District, for example, is a democratic body whose Com-

[1] A Petition for this has been in the hands of the Scottish Office since October 1935, and nothing has happened. Probably one of the main reasons why a Fishery District has not been established on the West Coast is that Inverness-shire and Argyll, the counties chiefly concerned, would have difficulty in financing it out of their low rateable value.

mittee consists of representatives from each fishing station in the area. The individual needs of each station and of every kind of fisherfolk, including lobstermen and cocklers, are considered in a personal and friendly way. A patrol vessel operates by day and night within the 3-mile limit to prevent poaching on the lobster-grounds, and to see that the Committee's bye-laws are properly observed.

With the trawlers gone and a local Fishery District Committee looking after the interests of the fishermen, it would be possible gradually to build up the industry to something like its former prosperity. It is impossible to say how long this would take, for the local line fishing has so nearly disappeared altogether that its revival might be a matter of considerable time. Probably after scientific observation and by general agreement certain areas would be set aside in which seining and trawling by small boats would be allowed at certain seasons.

The annual value of the shell-fish industry

in Scotland at the present time is upwards of £90,000 per annum, and there are those who consider that it might be greatly increased if suitable measures were adopted.

The complete revival of the local fishery would depend on faster and cheaper transport and much better arrangements for marketing than now exist. To expect such arrangements to be even started by the industry in its present state of collapse is to expect too much. This question of transport and marketing of course concerns the Highlands as a whole, and what Sir John Orr has proposed for Highland agriculture will apply, *mutatis mutandis*, to the fishing as well.

Special arrangements for the West Coast will include:

(1) Provision of refrigerating cars on the railways from Mallaig and Oban.

(2) Investigation of the commercial possibilities of

(*a*) transporting lobsters, scallops and cockles by air.

(*b*) The establishment of small-scale canning factories in Barra, etc.

(*c*) Refrigerating plant, either in the Islands or at the rail-head, whereby fish could be stored until a suitable quantity is ready for market.

(*d*) Revival in the export of sun-cured white fish to fish-eating countries in the Mediterranean and South America.

(3) Investigation of the methods of co-operation and transport employed in Norway with a view to their application here under similar geographical conditions.

(4) Speeding up of existing services, now no faster than they were fifty years ago. The steamer from Barra to Oban takes $11\frac{1}{2}$ to 12 hours.

(5) Provision of better communications between the Islands themselves. The posts are so slow that it is almost impossible to organise anything between the Islands, without

spending a small fortune on telegrams. People who go to the Islands for holidays only may see nothing wrong in this primitive state of affairs, but the regular inhabitants do and it is one of the factors tending to the depopulation of the Outer Isles.

Finally, there are required:

(1) Loans enabling fishermen to obtain boats on reasonable terms[1]; these would be a much safer investment if the Minch were closed to trawlers.

(2) Thorough scientific investigation of the potentialities of the waters of the Minch, and the demonstration and encouragement of suitable methods of fishing.* Decision on what areas could be used for trawling or seining by small boats, and the proper regulation of such trawling and seining.

---

[1] An appeal in *The Times* last January by Mr. Seton Gordon and others on behalf of lobstermen in Skye who had lost five boats in a storm and had no money to buy new ones, was extremely successful. Enough money was subscribed by the public, not only to buy the new boats but to provide a small fund for insurance against future disasters.

A MATTER FOR DECISION

If there were one single man whose job it was to look after Scotland, he would decide here and now whether the West Coast fisher-folk are wanted in Scotland. To keep them, he would force through Parliament before the next New Year's Day such measures as are outlined above. If the Westminster Parliament will not do it, Scotland must find a Parliament that will.

* Here is an example from Kintyre. In September 1936 at the instance of Colonel Campbell Galbraith, of Argyll Fisheries Ltd., clam (escollop) fishing was begun as a part-time occupation. In February of this year the *Campbeltown Courier* wrote as follows: ' The clam fishing which has been occupying the attention of local fishermen has been directly responsible for an improvement of conditions in the town. Dredges for the clam fishers are being manufactured locally by blacksmiths, while money has been put in circulation in the town from the revenue derived from the sale of the clams on the London market; practically the whole Clyde fishing fleet is now engaged in clam fishing. Boats from Campbel-town, Tarbert, Rothesay and the Ayrshire ports are finding it a profitable undertaking.' Clam fishing has also been successfully instituted off the coast of Skye.

CHAPTER VIII

RURAL INDUSTRIES

' Now, a man who makes a thing that is good in itself—it doesn't matter if it is a farm or a hearth-rug or a whale-bone seal—has asserted himself, and succeeded. He has effected something. And the sense of being ineffectual is one of the deepest roots of what is wrong with Scotland. It's at the bottom of much emigration, and it poisons Scots politics. Many an artisan has saved his soul by growing potatoes in an allotment. Now a craft that makes for skill, initiative, and honest pride, has the same effect, even if the economic value is almost nil. And Scotland needs pride—the right pride. She is suffering from a bad inferiority-complex, and that breeds hate.'

AGNES MURE MACKENZIE

ROME WAS not built in a day, and the slow-moving life of the Highlands will not be transformed overnight. Almost everything—good or bad—which happens in this world, is the result of one man's initiative, stimulated it may be and helped by a group of his friends, and in these years of mass-production and mass-propaganda we should remember this and take heart.

There are few places in Britain more suited for individual action and initiative than the Highlands. Historically, the Highlander has had to depend on himself for protection, for the means of life, and for all the services, such as medicine, education, transit, now provided by the State. Time was when the Highlander knew a path through the hills that he liked better than the public road. Now that is changed. New standards, new customs began to creep into the Highlands after 1746: the pace of the invasion has quickened of late years, and we find the Highlander crying out that he must have roads, telephones, postal services if his life is to be worth while. To an alarming extent he, who was the pattern of independence and self-reliance, has come to be dependent on the South. So much so that we find in winter, when the visitors from the South have gone back to the lights and cinemas of Piccadilly, the Highlander is living in idle darkness—in darkness because he is saving the cost of light and fire, and idle because there is nothing for him to do.

How can he be rescued in the winter evenings?

In the old times in the Glens there would be *ceilidhs*, which is Gaelic for musical parties or gatherings. But there would be more spontaneous mirth in the Highlands then, more young folk to justify it, and perhaps more money to support it. What of the present? Have the lights gone out and the songs been quieted in every glen?

Merriment will only be restored to the Highlands when there are more young folk there, and the only way to make sure of this is to put farming and fishing on a more extended basis in the Highlands with the direct object of increasing not only the food-supply but the man-supply of the Highlands. Sir John Orr, in the preceding chapters, has outlined this necessary policy. For its full success it must be supplemented by every possible effort on the part of the Highlanders themselves to increase and enrich their own means of life.

Research of course is needed, and still more a united spirit in Scotland to back that research, and make certain that it shall find what it is looking for. If the professional footballer is helped by playing before his own supporters, and hearing their cheers, scientists are human too, and even in their cold laboratories need the spur of appreciation. Scottish Nationalists tell us we need not expect much practical experimental work in Scotland from the British Government.

Has Scotland ever asked for such experimental work? Individuals or groups, yes, but the people, no. *Ask, and ye shall receive.* Carry your pitcher to the water, and you will bring it back full. The reason why so little advance is made in Scotland is that no one has yet put forward for Scotland a goal—what the

Greeks called τέλος, an end—which will *satisfy our whole being*. The want of such a goal is at the bottom of the whole Scottish problem. Neither the cry of Self-Government for Scotland, nor (in its more limited field) Mr. Quigley's Highland Development Board go deep enough to touch the human heart.

Science, at all events, must help us. Successful experiments have been made in Fascist Italy with a view to obtaining motor spirit from various waste matters. If Scots chemists could find a commercial value in bracken—*presto!* a pest removed and a rural industry created. So with peat, upon whose use as agricultural soil the Macaulay Institute has been researching for some time. In the Irish Free State the production of peat is an important rural industry. Peat is used by nearly every household in the Free State, and trials made by the Industrial Research Council on steam raising appliances and on a central heating installation show that peat can be used as a satisfactory fuel for these purposes. Further investigations by the Irish Government are in progress. The Shannon Hydro-Electric Power Scheme, which is controlled by the Irish Government, supplies cheap power to small villages as well as to towns. By contrast, peat and water-power lie almost wasted in the Highlands.

If once we could lay the foundations of a prosperous agriculture, we should not have to fear the effects of power stations; we should see only their undoubted benefits. The capital cost of making the power available at the low voltages required would admittedly be heavy, but it would be spent chiefly in wages to British workmen and the cost would be non-recurring; the power, once installed, would be a permanent national asset. With its help we could establish small industries in country places. The sons of farmers could then choose between industry and working on the land, without in either case having to leave the land. Such rural industries would of their nature be decentralised and opposed to monopoly, like the Galloway Tweed Mills referred to later in this chapter, and would wean from the cities many of our artisans who might shy at a plough. Skill and the tool-sense of our cities' artisans are a big part of Scotland's resources, and if we can avoid the crude defects of Industrial Capitalism there should be salvation in these little industries for many in our cities.

Scotland is probably the only part of Britain (unless it be Yorkshire) which combines at once the technical skill and the independent spirit required for this venture. It would be altogether a new step in the nation's life. It would have to be planned in conjunction with the Government, with a Government-guaranteed market for the first five years. But the initial impulse and the driving power would have to come from Scotland. Without such driving-power and a clear idea of what Scotland's general well-being requires, namely a better balance be-

tween town and country, the plan must fail,
for industry's whole tendency has been the
other way—to centralise, to form big companies and trusts. Local enterprise has got to
be extended, and it has got to be made
economic, or our civilisation will die like a
fish that cannot find its way back to the water.
To clear the road for such local enterprises,
Scots inventors must be encouraged; there
must be a list of Scots needs and problems
under constant organised research, not only
with the view of satisfying those needs and
problems, but of satisfying them in country
districts rather than in towns. The chance
of making a fortune sent many young Scotsmen
overseas in the last two centuries: the
avenues there are closing up. ' It is ', wrote
The Times Literary Supplement recently in
reviewing Professor Dewar Gibb's *Scottish
Empire*, ' It is an engaging vision that of the
Scot staying in Scotland and devoting to his
native land the energy and capacity that have
wrought so much change in other regions of

the globe. What the results of this change may be no man can tell.'

But agriculture will have to be served first. Any important development of rural industries, involving the transference of considerable numbers of artisans from the towns into the country, must await the re-establishment of agriculture on a secure and permanent basis. Meanwhile agriculture, like forestry and fishing, is a job which does not involve regular hours. All these pursuits leave some spare time, especially in the dark winter afternoons and evenings, for the countryman and his wife.

One such secondary occupation might well be found in individual craftsmanship. Reports have been issued from time to time on the question of expanding the few and, for the most part, scattered rural industries which already exist in Scotland. Much the most important of these is the tweed industry, centred in Harris and the Lews. The potential demand for hand-made Harris is much greater than the actual effective demand, represented by firm orders. What is wanted here is a more powerful publicity and selling organisation, of which the nucleus already exists in Highland Home Industries (see page 292). In the old days when Scotland had a King of her own it was just such a typically Scottish and individual industry as tweed-making that he would have sought to encourage: he would have promoted its sales both at home and in all the countries of Western Europe by his influence and energy, not for his own profit but *because the thing was good in itself, and Scottish*. What we want to awaken in Scotland now is the national will to support and promote all such enterprises as satisfy those two simple and sufficient conditions, and for that purpose there must eventually be established some organisation to give effect to that will of the people.

Galloway has several rug-making industries. To illustrate the kind of life they induce, I quote by permission of the Scottish B.B.C.

the following short account of Cree Mills, Newton Stewart which was given in the Everlasting Heritage Series a few months ago. The speaker, Mr. Hugh Galt, is the proprietor's son, who said:

' I believe that there is still a future for industry in country towns, especially in districts which attract tourists.' In reply to the question whether he found the tourist trade valuable, his answer was:

> Yes, very, and we set ourselves to make the most of it. Every year there are more and more tourists coming to Galloway, and most of them prefer a hand-made or distinctive article to the mass-produced stuff. Of course we in Galloway have the old tradition behind us. " Galloway for 'oo' " is still true, and it's very appropriate because a large percentage of Scottish wool is grown in Galloway. We ourselves buy wool direct from local farms and process it right to the finished article.

Asked whether he liked Galloway, he replied:

> Very much indeed. The country round Newton Stewart is very fine. In fact we get most of our ideas for our colour schemes from the changing

seasons in the valleys behind the town. My father often goes into the glens with a great variety of different coloured wools and blends them and mixes them until he strikes on something new which the scene inspires, an autumn mixture for example, with something for the bright leaves and the grey stones and so on.

Asked how country workmen compare with men in a town, he replied:

Well, as a rule there is only one industry in a small country town, so that people are more interested in their work. They take a local pride and a family interest in the business as it were. On the other hand, town workmen have better facilities for technical education.

You would like to see these facilities extended to the country?

Yes, and I would like to see industry less centralised, less completely organised for the production of millions of things all alike. The small industry in the country town can afford to make a variety of things, and if the people in charge of small industries don't go to sleep, but are alert and eager and enterprising, I don't see why the big towns should beat them and take all their work from them.

But, Mr. Galt, there is just this one point. Will you get people to stay in the small villages and towns? Will you have attractions enough to keep them there?

> You can make the small towns attractive by foot-
> ball, golf, lawn-tennis, amateur theatricals, cinemas
> —and things like that.

Here, then, we have a flash of the will that
can—the evidence of a man who owns and
runs a successful rural industry in Galloway,
and through local agents does a large business
with the summer tourists besides selling to
the big cities of Britain, to America, Canada,
South Africa, and Australia.

This mill employs between fifty and sixty
people the whole year round, and could
employ more if there were more local labour
available, for ' it's all we can do ', he says,
' to supply the demand.' The mill is on the
banks of the Cree, and water for scouring,
dyeing, and heating comes from the river.
Most of the machinery is driven by electricity
from the national grid.

Let us now turn and look at a small town in
the Highlands—Oban. In evidence given
before the Sub-Committee of the Economic
Committee of the Scottish Development

Council last November, Mr. Black, the Town Clerk, said that ' the main, one may almost say the only, industry of Oban is the tourist one ', which swells the normal population of 5,600 to about 15,000 in the first fortnight of August. He went on to say that it is far from easy to suggest how and what sort of a new industry could be organised in Oban.

It would seem on the face of it that Oban and its neighbourhood have a magnificent opening for small rural industries to manufacture good-class Highland articles for sale to tourists. Such articles are manufactured and freely sold in Switzerland and the Black Forest.

Here is a chance for one man's initiative to show itself. It need not be on a large scale to begin with, nor involve much capital: all it requires is patience in the long winter evenings, craftsmanship and some technical training in the first place by experts in the various crafts. A local character would soon be given to their work by the Highland craftsmen themselves. To take a single example out of many, the tourist's delight in old Scottish castles and other romantic places might be exploited by the manufacture of small wooden replicas of Dunstaffnage and Dunolly Castles. If these replicas were well made at the start and the fashion pleased the public, it would spread all over Scotland, providing spare-time winter employment to craftsmen in cottages from Sutherland to Galloway. Such an industry would have the special advantage of spreading some knowledge of Scottish Architecture both among those who made and those who bought the replicas.

Once such a trade were in being, it would be easy to feel the pulse of the public, and to adapt designs accordingly. ' Hand-made in the Highlands ', ' Hand-made in the Borders ', or ' in Galloway ', should be the purchaser's guarantee that he was getting what he wanted, namely an article of individuality with a local character.

HANDICRAFTS FOR TOURISTS

So short a book as this cannot hope to cover the whole ground, but here are two illuminating suggestions put forward by Miss Bruce, of Highland Home Industries.

In all Highland industries I would recommend a closer connection with the Forestry Commission whose workers could be trained in various wood crafts which would find a good market in the Company's Depots.

An industry which should be encouraged in Skye is the cutting and polishing of the really beautiful stones found on the Island. These could be set in artistic designs and would find a ready sale among the tourists. This remark refers to practically the whole of the Highlands. There does not appear to be a single lapidary in Scotland and I think if one or two men were trained in this work they would find full time occupation. Under careful guidance these stones could be set in a variety of beautiful designs and to people of taste would form an attractive memento of their visit to Scotland.

Rural industries in Scotland are said to have been seriously handicapped in the past by two things: the lack of technical instructors, and unwillingness among the craftsmen to pool their products for sale. Wayside stalls, for the sale of dairy and garden produce and handicrafts, especially to tourists, have been started recently in Berwickshire with the encouragement of the Scottish Agricultural Organisation Society and the Scottish Women's Rural Institutes. This example might well be followed on a co-operative basis in the Highlands when rural industries have been developed there.

Technical instruction in some crafts is now being disseminated by the Women's Rural Institutes, but no flourishing rural industry appears to have arisen out of their activities, save that in Shetland, where knitting forms the chief means of livelihood for most of the women, the Scottish W. R. I. have helped them to sell the greater part of their work. It would seem desirable to give instruction equally to the men, and to make them realise that what is meant is business, with a direct potential effect on the annual income. The cultural advantages of such a spare-time occupation might be allowed to penetrate the mind by what Andrew Kirkcaldy in another connection called the kitchen-door.

Once it is seen that Scottish rural craftsmen meant business, and were prepared to take the opportunity with both hands, a body like the Pilgrim Trust might not impossibly furnish the means to provide a number of trained instructors, who would travel up and down the glens, founding what would be really a School of National Craftsmanship.

This is the age of locomotion, and we must expect tourists more and more. Why should we not, in this way among others, plan to increase at once their pleasure and our own security in the Highlands and the Lowlands of our home?

II

An interesting experiment on these lines is being made in the Lowlands. A body known officially as Scottish Country Industries Development Trust, and familiarly as S. C. I. D was started a year ago. Its office is 111a George Street, Edinburgh, and it works in conjunction with Highland Home Industries, of the same address, but unlike H. H. I., is not a trading concern. It is a purely advisory body. It receives at present through the Department of Agriculture in Scotland an annual grant of £1700 which enables it to maintain, besides a small staff at headquarters, one local Organizer in Galloway. The Trust is assisted by the Rural Industries Bureau in London. The Bureau has sent instructors and designers to help the Trust and it is hoped ultimately that the Trust may through an increased grant obtain men of similar qualifications for Scotland permanently.

A preliminary survey in the counties of Dumfries, Wigtown and Kirkcudbright was made by Ian Macpherson over a period of two and a half months last year. He has kindly allowed me to see a copy of his Report, from which the following facts and figures are taken.

348 tradesmen were visited in the three counties:

Blacksmiths	180
Joiners	109
Millwrights	2
Iron workers other than smiths	7
Saddlers	11
Millers	4
Wool Manufacturers	8
Clogmakers	9
Arty Craftsmen	1
Builders	2
Sculptors	1
Bobbin Manufacturers	5
Quarriers	2
Tanners	2
Beekeepers	1
Lime Kilns	1
Brick and Tile Manufacturers	3
	348

What help can the Trust give? It is illuminating that Mr. Macpherson, who is a practical man and likes to keep his feet firmly on the ground, yet reports that the best help which the Trust can give is to restore the countryman's confidence in himself. He says:

> If the Trust succeeds in helping country trades and industries to be more efficient so that they regain trade they have almost lost, it is not the material results that are most important. Men who cannot keep themselves alive in their accustomed occupations lose their self-respect. If they are assisted to make, advertise, and sell tradesmanlike work, they will regain their self-respect, which is more important than the goods they produce, or the money they are paid for producing them. To help and encourage men to use their skill producing useful or beautiful things, is to bring a little stability into the uneasy country.

The superior prestige of the towns, to which we refer elsewhere in this book, was found to have had two effects in Galloway. It made the rural tradesman despair of competing against factory work, and it caused some snobbish farmers to buy their carts and henhouses from large firms in a town, simply because the firms were large and advertised expensively, whereas better-made carts and henhouses could have been had at a lower price from the local joiner.

Bureaucracy and the desire to save trouble in the office, have led County Councils to buy tools from ' a huge firm in Sheffield ' rather than support the local men from whom they collect the rates.

The farmer's snobbery, the joiner's inferiority-complex, and the unfairness of officials can best be countered by the pressure of local opinion. And this opinion can most effectively be aroused by a local Organiser working on behalf of a national body known to be vigilant, sympathetic and strong. The influence of prestige is a thing which cannot be measured, but when the rural craftsman knows that against unfair treatment he can appeal to the representative of a national body, the mere knowledge of this may give him a confidence which will make the appeal itself unnecessary. Rural Community Councils, of which there are unfortunately at present only two in Scotland (Kirkcudbrightshire and Angus), can do much to help, and so can the local lairds and other people of influence in each district.

A countryman believes, not what he is told, but what he sees. The best way to convince him that a thing is good is to let him see it at work. He will believe in the Trust so soon as it helps himself or someone in his neighbourhood. That is why, in order to prevent disillusionment, it is important that results should follow fast upon the survey, and also why a survey and results in one area should be swiftly followed by a survey and results in another.

The technique of farming has changed, and country tradesmen if they are to keep their old place in the rural community, must learn new technique too. ' A great many men who can with our help ', says Mr. Macpherson, ' accommodate themselves to modern conditions would without assistance, slowly go under.'

HOW THE TRUST CAN HELP

The value of propaganda on behalf of rural industries needs no underlining. One short paragraph in Mr. Macpherson's gloomy report explains why millers in the South West are vanishing. ' Millers ', he says, ' provide very little scope for assistance so long as the public is incapable of telling good oatmeal from bad.'

' Look at me ', said a young farm labourer in Lanarkshire; ' I eat porridge fourteen times a week.' He abides by the old pre-scription, and thrives on it, none the worse that the oats are grown on his father's fields, and ground by the miller half a mile up the country road.

The best way to persuade the rural crafts-man that he can compete against the factory is to make him do it. Apart from general propaganda, the Trust can help the individual in these ways:

I By giving business help in buying, costing, pricing, estimating, book-keeping, advertising, selling—and debt collecting.

II By suggesting ideas and showing designs of saleable articles.

III By giving technical advice.

IV By arranging exhibitions and Sales.

An alert and skilful craftsman who takes advantage of these services will soon convince himself that he *can* beat the factory, and once he has discovered this, he will stand on his own feet. As the open-air movement has shown, there is a widespread longing nowadays (curiously co-incident with the drift to the towns) to escape from the machine and its limitations, and one sign of this is the demand for hand-made quality productions, a demand which with a little encouragement could be enormously increased. Country joiners who are keen on this class of work and will train themselves for it, need fear no lack of commissions: a joiner in Dumfriesshire who specialises on bog-oak reading-lamps, folding tables, elm porridge-bowls, etc., has orders on hand to occupy him for months

ahead.[1]   In the summer-tourist districts,
again, there is a special opening for summer
houses, garden seats and porches; all these can
and should be made by local joiners.

The plan put forward last July by the Com-
missioner for the Special Areas of Scotland to
build single-storey houses of timber, in order
to counteract the present shortage of brick-
layers and plasterers will depend for its
success very largely on the available supply of
joiners.   If it becomes a success, the fashion
would soon spread to the rural areas, for timber houses are more attractive features of a
country landscape than houses made of brick;
the country joiner would therefore be wise to
prepare himself for such work, which would go
far to solve the twin problems of rural housing
and of employment for rural tradesmen.

The country tradesman, be he craftsman

[1] I asked him why he did not train an apprentice, and he replied
that the young folks had not the necessary patience.   This is part
of the whole great question of making country life ' worth while ',
both spiritually and financially, to the younger generation which
quite rightly is in the mood to expand.

or shop-keeper, cannot flourish alone. His prosperity must depend ultimately on the prosperity of the farmer, who should be taught to look upon the tradesman as his business partner. Land given over to sheep farming supports no trades, and the dairy farming country along the Galloway coast and beside the rivers gives little support to smiths and joiners, because the soil is soft and horses' shoes and other agricultural implements last a long time without repair. It is the intermediate farming area between the hills and the plain, suited for stock breeding and rearing, that gives work to the ancillary trades, and when Mr. Morrison's proposals for the recovery of the livestock industry have taken shape, these rural trades will recover also.

But the farmer and the tradesman need not wait on Mr. Morrison. They can do something at once to help themselves.[1] They

[1] In one village of Upper Clydesdale, for example, the joiner's son has built up a valuable business in haulage—first of sheep and cattle, then of coal also, and this led to his becoming the local coal merchant.

might enlarge each other's incomes if they
would sit down together in the long autumn
evenings and plan to give a proper country
welcome to the holiday-makers in Galloway
next summer. Mr. Macpherson's report on
the conditions he found in one village in 1936
is astonishing.

This village, with several hundred residents all
the year round, and a large summer population, has
no joiner, and no smith; its bakery does no baking
but gets its bread and cakes three times a week
from Glasgow via the country town. The Butcher
supplies certain kinds of meat, only on certain days a
week. The consequence is firstly that the Hotels
get their provisions from the nearest town. The
village life is thereby impoverished. And secondly,
the hotels are liable to actual famine, as at Easter
when they ran short of food, and could not get any
in their country towns because it was the monthly
whole holiday. But what is more important, the
town people who come to this village have country
air and the country scene to refresh them, but of
country food, fresh good farm butter and eggs and
cream, country baking and country meat, there is
none. They eat the same things as they eat in
Glasgow, only not so fresh after their journey from
Glasgow. And of course of country vegetables
newly grown and cooked, of such fruits as can be

grown in the South West, of flowers for hotel rooms from local gardens—there is nothing at all.

Who is to set the ball rolling? Fine words butter no parsnips, and a depressed countryside will not exert itself for its own advantage without being encouraged by a lead. It is precisely here that a resident Organiser, and/ or a Rural Community Council on the spot, can help. People who think that no scheme for social reconstruction is any good until its practical application has been worked out to the last detail, do not use their imagination enough. They forget that the practical application must match the moods of a moody race, and that the approach to be successful, must be made not only in the right way but at the right moment. Hence the value of a man on the spot, able to understand the special capacities and the special aptitudes of the people of his own district.

That the work of Scottish Country Industries Development Trust is appreciated is evident, not only directly in Galloway where an Organiser is established, but from the enquiries which reach the Head Office from other parts of Scotland: 'You are helping the South West. When are you coming to help us in Perthshire?'

III

The tourist industry is the most important rural industry in the Highlands during the summer season. What help does it give to the local farmers and fishermen? A friend of mine who was travelling on the West Coast for a few days last June told me that the food he was given in several Highland hotels on that visit consisted principally of bread from Glasgow (he told me the name of the firm that made it), sour butter, cheese packets and chocolate wrapped in tinfoil. This does not suggest a close association between hotel-keeper and Highland farmer. By contrast, Acharacle Hotel, near the foot of Loch Shiel, supplied my friend with good local food in which his soul (as well as his body) delighted:

he felt that here he was being not only fed, but hospitably entertained.

After stressing the need that food should be *fresh*, Professor Stapledon writes.[1]

> There is another very important aspect of the food problem and that is its local significance. There are two sides to this question, firstly, that of extreme freshness, and secondly, the interest and relish that follow upon the eating locally of an essentially local product. . . . Local products are lost every year. . . . At least it should be possible for the townsman going to the country for holidays to be able to obtain fresh meat, fresh milk, fresh eggs, fresh vegetables produced within a stone's throw of wherever he may stay or take his meals.

The spirit, if not the letter, of this pronouncement is observed by the Proprietor of the Red Lion Hotel, Petersfield, in Hampshire. On his Menus you read ' Salmon and lobsters supplied to this hotel direct from Dornoch Firth.' I asked him how he managed it. He orders a 20 lb. salmon to come by the train leaving Bonar Bridge at 12 noon. The fisherman, who knows him personally,

[1] *The Hill Lands of Britain* (Faber and Faber), p. 118.

knocks the salmon on the head about an hour before, so it is sent off fresh and reaches Petersfield by train next day at 12.36 p.m. Cooked and served the same evening, it is fresher than you would get in most south-country hotels; and provides for the hotel guests that 'interest and relish' of which Professor Stapledon speaks.

> I have the satisfaction of knowing that I am serving the genuine article and am complimented on it dozens of times in a year. This means that people come back again and again, and what is better still they tell their friends to do likewise.

The arrangement saves the hotel-keeper money, too: every fish that he has had from Bonar Bridge has saved him at least fourpence per lb. net; sometimes the saving has been as much as eightpence per lb., although the local fishmonger would have given him favourable terms. His supplier pays the carriage, and he has no empties to send back. He orders the salmon by post-card or if necessary by wire, and he always receives a fish weighing more than he ordered, but he is charged only for what he stated in lbs. One 20-pounder weighed 26¾ lbs. and he received a bill for 20 lbs. of salmon at 1/5 per lb!

His lobsters come from Portmahomack on the Dornoch Firth, and connect at Tain with the same mail train bringing the salmon from Bonar Bridge. He buys lobsters a dozen at a time. They are wrapped in damp sawdust, and reach him alive. Usually there are eleven of about a pound and a half, and one biggish one of about two and a half or three pounds, a very suitable lobster out of which to make lobster salads. His invoice always reads the same,

12 lobsters at 1/6 each	18	0
Carriage	3	3

and it costs him a further 1/10 to return the empty box.

I made personal contact with my suppliers (said the hotel-keeper) when I was staying up in Ross-shire about 3 years ago, and I always make a point of seeing them when I go North. I also make a point of sending my cheque the day I receive my account and I always send them a Christmas Card.

Now let us see what help is given to these North of Scotland fishermen by hotel-keepers in Sutherland and Ross-shire. In a broadcast talk last May on ' Transport in Scotland ' Mr. Hugh Macrae, the manager of a transport company operating in Sutherland, said that the tourist traffic ' is of no value to the agricultural and fishing communities ' except to a crofter or fisherman who gets a few weeks' work as a ghillie at the local hotel.

Even the local merchant reaps very little benefit from them, because the hotel keeper, who must run his establishment on the most up-to-date and economic lines, gets his supplies wholesale from the big city stores, while fresh milk, eggs and vegetables are provided by his own croft or farm. Many hotel proprietors, besides, own a number of sheep, and supply their own mutton. . . . So tourist traffic, as we know it at present, offers no solution to the major problem of agriculture and fishing, which are the life blood of the Highlands.

How much more ' up-to-date ' would be the hotel bread if it were baked locally instead of coming hundreds of miles from a store in Glasgow! Some Highland hotels use tinned vegetables and even the chickens are not always Highland birds. This dependence on the towns, though to some extent and in some places at present unavoidable, is not only ruining the small local producers where these still exist, but also frustrates, as Macpherson and Stapledon both agree, the whole purpose of the townsman's holiday which is to provide him with a change—change of air, change of scene, change of food! Highland hotels are popularly supposed to be expensive: many of them, if they bought more of their supplies from local men, would be buying both well and cheaply. It would require of course a little organisation, and also a little human sympathy for the people among whom they live. To allow the crofter-fishermen around them gradually to fade away is suicidal: it must mean in the long run the decline of the whole district, including the hotels, for transport and other amenities will never be provided for the Highlands on the scale that hotel-keepers and garage men would like, unless there is a local population to reap the benefit of such improvements. If wider roads and cheaper rail fares are only going to mean flooding the district with more and more supplies from big city stores, to the increasing detriment of local producers—then the Government will decline to put down public money for that purpose.

IV

If rural industry were established on a sound footing in the Highlands, it would do more than help to keep the crofters going in the winter. For the satisfaction of creative work is much more than the cash which it brings in, welcome as this may be to supplement the family earnings. Mr. Baldwin said recently that craftsmanship, which was once the pride of Britain, has been largely superseded by the minding of machines: the individual act of creative construction gives place to watching

179

the endless repetition of the same mechanical processes, month after month. These conditions do not yet apply over the whole field of industry: many of the Clyde engineers, for example, still taste the joy of creative craftsmanship in their work, although their lives otherwise—their homes and their amusements—have become standardised as one of them, Edward Shiels, has shown in his novel *Gael over Glasgow*. But wherever industry is able to replace craftsmen by a machine it does so, and scientific discovery is enabling it to do so in some new field every week. When the fever of industrialism has run its course, the men of a new age will wonder what was our object in building so many factories, and will visit their gaunt interiors as we visit Stonehenge or the Temples of Greece, marvelling at some *meaning* which must once have prompted their erection, but which is quite hidden from us now.

' Many of our troubles to-day ', Mr. Baldwin continued, ' seem to me to be due to the

growing materialism of the age we live in.
. . . Materialism means slavery of the mind
to the things of the body, and slavery in the
end means destruction.'

From this slavery, as we have seen in Chapter II, Scotland stands in great danger, and
the cure for it is precisely that vigorous,
independent life which by tradition and geo-
graphy the Highlands are particularly well
fitted to provide. Rural industries, if developed and made to flourish up and down the
Highlands, would not only help Scotland
indirectly by contributing to the revival of
her largest district, but would everywhere
encourage that craftsman spirit of personal
creation which a man needs if his life is to be
full, and the want of which is perhaps the
deepest cause of our unhappiness to-day.

In the old days almost everything the Highlander did, from his fighting and his music to
his fishing and crofting, had this quality of
personal impact, and he thrived on it. In the
towns food is something that you buy from

the baker, or the grocer. But the Highlander wants to see the corn spring, from which he will eat the bread. He wants to make the song which will bring tears to a girl's eye. And he wanted to see the sword go in, to make a corpse that should not fight again. He is not content, as a man in a factory has to be content, to go through the motions without seeing the result.

Now if such a deep-seated craving is persistently frustrated, a sense of futility follows, made worse in the West Highlands by the Atlantic climate which disposes to lassitude and melancholy. Clan feuds made a fine antidote,[1] and there was more music then.

[1] The other side is expressed in this comment: ' Was there anything fine about clan feuds? The six years Campbell-MacLean war on Mull, for instance, must have been hell. It's only in countries like 16th century Scotland and 16th century Spain where everyone prated of ' the honour of a gentleman ' that these incredible parricides and fratricides and filicides (if that's the right word) occurred. The loyalty of the Highlanders was real enough but so was their treachery. On second thoughts, there are two things that are striking: the loyalty of the clansmen to their leaders and the treachery of these leaders to each other and, after the forfeited estates were restored, to their own clansmen.'

Now there are no antidotes, and the effect of the climate has been increased in some parts of the Islands by religious hysteria. To make up the tally of distresses, the Highlander responds to and needs leadership, and whereas under the clan system he had it, under the system of sporting landlords living in England he doesn't get it—and so gradually the soul of the Highlander has been dying. Besides putting agriculture on a sound basis, and promoting rural industries, provision will have to be made in one form or another for personal leadership, not from England but from a Scotsman dwelling in the glen and if possible a member of the clan. He would use his knowledge and influence to find markets both for his people's agricultural produce and their industrial crafts: the unwillingness to co-operate which observers have noticed in parts of the Highlands, is due to petty suspicions which a trusted leadership would very soon dissolve.

The Highlands indeed are ripe for development, but on three conditions: that agriculture and fishing shall be served first: that the new industries to be introduced shall be individual small-town or cottage industries, in whose products the workmen and their womenfolk can take a local pride and interest: and thirdly that leadership—not necessarily as under the old clan system, but a personal leadership as between man and man, such as the Scots everywhere understand—shall return to the glens.

CHAPTER IX

RURAL AMENITIES

' The difference between our country dances and these Scottish figures is about the same as leisurely stirring a cup o' tea and beating up a batter-pudding. I was extremely gratified to think that, if I had pleasures they knew nothing of, they had also some into which I could not possibly enter. I hope I shall not return without having got the Highland fling. There was as fine a row of boys and girls as you ever saw; some beautiful faces, and one exquisite mouth. I never felt so near the glory of Patriotism, the glory of making by any means a country happier. This is what I like better than scenery.'

KEATS

ALL THE activities of life are inspired ultimately by Desire. When Dante ended his *Paradiso* with the line

The Love that moves the sun and the other stars

he was probably thinking of how Aristotle described the Creator, κινεῖ ὡς ἐρώμενον,

' He moves the world as One that is loved.'
And this great truth is confirmed, as great
truths often are, by our own experience, by
the simple animal desires for food and shelter
to preserve life, and for self-reproduction to
preserve the life of the race. Desire has
become a word of debased coinage. We use
it now to point a contrast with Duty, as
though the instinct of Duty were not itself
the expression of some longing deep within us.

As a tree unconsciously aspires to grow
straight and tall and to spread wide its
branches, so a man more and more consciously desires to fulfil his nature, which
implies—not as the goal but as a sort of visa
permitting him to travel—the observance of
a moral law.

' With desire ', said Christ to his disciples,
' I have desired to eat this passover with you
before I suffer.' That was the sublimation of
what we should call in our own place both
Desire and Duty. It fulfils the ideal which
Plato propounded for education, φιλεῖν ἃ δεῖ

φιλεῖν, that we children shall 'love what we ought to love', as indeed it is natural we should: and not by the grey process of clipping Desire's wings until she droops to her mate Duty on the ground, but by giving to Duty the wings of Desire so that they become no more two but one, and the bird rises to the golden light. Only so shall we satisfy our inmost being, and—we need not doubt—the purpose of our Maker.

It is within this context that a re-peopling of the Highlands must be considered. For though a national duty, it is also capable of stirring Desire to a very high degree, both individually and nationally.

Until, however, individuals and the Scottish people as a whole are moved by that desire so strongly as to make the Highlands once more a home and not a mere playground, no amount of political manoeuvring, no speeches and no pamphlets will ever do it. To awake the Sleeping Beauty of Desire what is wanted is a Prince Charming, whose name and identity are as yet unrevealed: exponents of moral indignation, however well-intentioned, will knock at the castle door in vain. Until the common man wants it, and until Scotland wants it, the Government cannot be expected to tackle the problem in earnest. Therefore the first step is for Scotland and individual Scots to express an active desire that the Highlands shall become a home of our race.

There is no doubt that such a desire exists, but it has become buried by hopelessness and by the distraction of other interests. Hopelessness will disappear very quickly when the thing is found to be realisable, and the other interests of Scotland and Scotsmen have not proved so completely satisfying that we are yet a contented people. We are, in fact, a deeply dissatisfied and uncertain people in Scotland. We have at present no idea where the future is taking us, except that it will take—unless we rule otherwise—a great many more of us furth of Scotland.

THE INDIVIDUAL'S DESIRE

The natural and perhaps the deepest desire of every Scot is to have a secure footing in his native land. To become a landowner, in a big or a small way, has always been the ambition of a Scot, and many of us besides have felt, with Rob Roy MacGregor, that we were only then our true selves when we had our foot upon our native heath.

Scots of course are proverbial for their success in other lands. The Colonies provided many openings which our race was quick to fill, and nowadays the increasing centralisation of business still brings many of us to the South. This fact, which is due primarily to the same economic pull as is tending to empty the North of England, does not lessen a deep and ineradicable desire to draw our strength from the Scottish hills, to live there if we could, and to give—wherever life may lead us—our best to Scotland. This feeling constitutes a silent reservoir of service ready for a statesman to tap. If the lead were given, as it will be given, by a Scot of brains, independence and the power of inspiration, there is a people waiting to follow.

But to give a lead before some of the necessary conditions are provided, is not the part of a statesman, and if our Desire is to be fulfilled it must be satisfied not only in the general, but in the particular as well. More particularly, many might say, in the particular! General ideas of a nation arising to a fuller life are of no use without food, drink, comfortable houses, means of travel, posts, telephones, schools, playgrounds, and enough neighbours to provide dances, music and all kinds of sport and games for the young, and recreation and gossip for the old folk.

Here is a bunch of indispensables to begin with and the man who is going to release in Scotland a practical desire for the re-peopling of the Highlands must see the way clear to a good many at least of these amenities before he appears upon the public stage.

And who will provide these essentials? We have grown so used to saying that ' the

Government ' must be our nurse, that we have got out of the way of remembering that we can do a lot of things for ourselves.

The first need, as I see it, is for enthusiasm —a real desire that this thing shall come to pass: the second need, as suggested in Chapter IV, is that the Government should demonstrate their determination to make agriculture in the Highlands pay: the third need will be to provide those amenities without which even the natural desire to make a home on Scots soil could hardly hold out against the fleshpots of Glasgow.

Individual enterprise can do a great deal, but it cannot in these days supply public services such as the hill-roads which are wanted by the people of Moidart, the increased posts and the telephones required in the Outer Isles, or the agricultural training which is needed for boys and girls up and down the Highlands to-day. Nor can individual enterprise build all the houses that will be wanted, nor village-halls and play-grounds where these are not already available.[1] For such purposes public money will plainly be required.

Now if instead of casting all our burdens upon Whitehall, we were to regard this problem as a national one for Scotland—which it is—and were to raise by voluntary subscription a Loan for the Development of the Highlands on the assumption that the Government would provide £1 for every £1 subscribed by Scotland—if we made such a proposal to Mr. Elliot, on assurances that the scheme would be efficiently managed and would be *driven through* by the Scottish people's enthusiasm and Mr. Elliot's driving power jointly, I believe that this offer would be accepted by the Government and that we should quickly begin to see satisfactory results. In that enterprise every Scot would find a practical outlet for his patriotism, and those who could not contribute in cash and yet wished to help,

[1] Grants and loans towards the building of Village Halls are provided, under certain conditions, by the Carnegie United Kingdom Trust. Such grants were promised during 1936 to seven villages in Scotland, of which six were in the Highlands.

could enrol for short spells of land improvement work, such as bracken-cutting which needs to be undertaken in the Highlands on a big scale. Once it was seen that Scotland was embarked whole-heartedly on the development and re-population of the Highlands, the unemployed would be absorbed—practically and mentally—in the job, and Scotland would have gone a long way to save herself by her exertions, and the rest of Great Britain by her example.

If we go on blaming and belittling one another's efforts, the house of Scotland is bound to fall. If rather we unite in sacrifice and labour for a cause which links us with our past history, with our children's prospects in life, and with each other—then there is hope, and more than hope, for Scotland.

It must, however, be remembered that the immediate object of all this effort would be to make the Highlands a home for more and more of our people. Suitable candidates there would be in plenty, once the attraction of the new amenities were made known, and the only fear is that in the excitement of 'development', enthusiasm might be allowed to out-run itself. There is point in what St. Paul said to the prison-sergeant. The prison-sergeant was proud of his newly-acquired Roman citizenship, which he had bought 'at a great price': St. Paul, the unconsidered prisoner, replied, 'But I was born free.' He had the citizenship by birth. The birth-right of the Highlands is their peace and natural beauty, and nothing that money can buy will ever give us anything so good, nor can money restore that birthright to us if we should be so mad as to destroy it. It does not belong to us: it is a heritage that has come from our fathers, and we hold it in trust for our sons.

To enlarge on the peculiar value of that amenity is difficult, and perhaps not worth while: people who are urban-minded do not know the language of the hills, and anyone who does is admitted at once into their

mystery which it would be mere impertinence
in me to try to expound. But I may borrow
a sentence from Sir John Sutherland's broadcast talk on National Parks: after telling us
that Cecil Rhodes used to withdraw to the
mountain-tops of Africa to commune with
himself, and that Smuts went to the same
place to commune with God, he said: ' There
is no finer environment for clear thinking
and the comprehension of great ideals than
among the high hills.' Who that knows them
would deny it?

Surely in that environment we would wish
our sons and daughters to spend their early
years—the mind and spirit open to those
noble influences, and the body hardened and
helped to grow up strong by the air of the
hills, by healthy simple food, and by vigorous
and happy exercise. For among the amenities
which the Highlands already offer are a
thousand natural playgrounds in the glens and
by the shores of loch and ocean: mountain-
paths for riding: streams and lochs to fish in:

hunting in the hills: and on the lochs swimming, sailing and rowing.

It has been well said that in the towns you buy your pleasures, in the country you make them. Was there ever a finer place in which to make them than the Highlands of Scotland?

II

However desirable in itself, the mere extension of rural amenities will not be enough to re-people the Highlands, or indeed any part of rural Scotland. The rock-bottom necessity is confidence on the farmer's part that the Government is going to go on seeing him through. If for instance Scots farmers had any reason to fear that the guaranteed price for oats, which the Government has recently announced, were to be dropped, confidence would go too and the rural population would decline still further. Townspeople do not readily understand why the farmer needs the Government's constant support. The reason is that agriculture is not an industry which makes large profits—as may be seen from the low wage paid to farm labourers: few town-workers, skilled or un-skilled, would look cheerfully at 31/- a week. If the farmer raised prices high enough to pay his men a wage of 40/-, the cost of food would go up and the towns would order a retreat. To that extent agriculture in this country must always be depressed, and to maintain even a tolerable standard of living for its workers, it needs a certain degree of artificial stimulation.

If Sir John Orr's proposals are adopted, country folk will bear an easy mind. They will look forward to the future with confi-dence, and it is only in that atmosphere that any important extension of rural amenities can be successfully launched. These ameni-ties fall into two kinds, occupational and recreational.

To the first class belong all those things which a country worker—farmer, shepherd, ploughman, joiner—needs for carrying on his job. Besides food and drink (which are not amenities) he needs a dry, well-aired, well-lit house; he needs a rough road by which a car or at least a motor-bicycle can reach the house; he needs water for washing and sanitation; and he needs access to a telephone.

Rural cottages in Scotland are frequently dark, airless and cramped. Mr. Elliot has said that from his knowledge there are inhabited houses in Glasgow worse than any in the country. He is doing all that one man can do to remedy this disgrace. Some day every cottage in Scotland will have water and electricity laid on, and will be dry, well-aired and spacious, with proper arrangements for sanitation. All this must be part of the goal we aim at in planning the Scotland of our sons.

Not only the farm-houses and cottages, but the farm buildings, must be made weather-tight, sanitary and roomy. As the Minister for Scotland said: ' We have got to get the beasts healthy,' and the byres must be made fit for healthy beasts.

HILL FARMERS

A shepherd's wife from the hills walked into New Galloway last spring. It was the first time she had seen another woman for six months. Few are the women, or the men, nowadays, who would be content with so rare a privilege.

Hill farmers and hill shepherds are great people, and hill districts have long been strongholds of human worth. How many of the best lowland farmers have not migrated from or been born in the hills? And it is not only great farmers who have been born and nurtured on the hills. I regard the depopulation of hill districts as a serious national matter, and far indeed from being only of local significance—a matter that calls for national action.[1]

The motor bus has helped country life enormously by linking up the outlying villages with each other and with the country town, but buses cannot afford to wander in pursuit of far-off shepherds. Wireless has taken the edge off a shepherd's loneliness, but it has also widened his world; if he and his wife are young, the Scots dance music coming over the

[1] *The Land Now and To-morrow* by R. G. Stapledon (Faber and Faber), p. 224.

air makes them long to be flinging their steps with the others down in the village hall. No mother in these days wants to be out of reach of the doctor, and many a shepherd's cottage is miles from a metalled road. Professor Stapledon would meet this changed situation by a re-grouping of houses and hamlets in outlying places, to bring them within the orbit of the village, and he recommends especially the creation of what he calls ' track roads ', i.e. roads good enough to carry a car and motor-cycle in all weathers. Such roads could follow the old hill-tracks in many parts of Scotland.

Some people may find it difficult to understand why rough roads of this kind have not already been begun in outlying districts where they are wanted, by the local people instead of sending complaints to the Ministry of Transport. It would be coals of fire in the old Highland style. As Bailie Nicol Jarvie rejoined when accused of having insured his cattle *contra bonos mores*, ' If the law canna protect my barn and byre, what for suld I no engage wi' a Hieland gentleman that can? Answer me that.' Where the inhabitants made a start for themselves, the Ministry of Transport (one would think) would soon be shamed into sending professionals to complete the job.

One would need however to be very young indeed to think anything of the kind. For years in the Outer Isles the inhabitants have had to make and repair roads because otherwise the work would simply not have been done. Motorists in Barra have lately refused to pay road licence fees and so contribute to a Road Fund which contributed nothing to Barra roads. This is not the first sign that Government in the far parts of Scotland has begun to break down.

The whole question of transport, especially in the West, must be drastically handled as a part of the problem of making life tolerable on a modern standard for men and women in the Highlands and Islands. Transport and communications are much more than an amenity: they are part of the economic framework. If it costs (as it does cost) a farmer in North Uist twice as much to ship eggs from Lochmaddy to Fort William as it costs to send them from Shetland to Edinburgh, that makes poultry-keeping in the Outer Isles so much the more difficult. That is a typical difficulty of life in the West Highlands, and it has got to be overcome. The people of the Outer Isles and of the West and North-West have to be brought into the family circle, and not just left to get along as best they can on the boundaries of the kingdom.

Where a pier is needed to enable the steamer to make a daily call, as at Glenelg in the narrows opposite Skye, a pier must be built. The crofters of Glenelg, a valley almost inaccessible by road, need fertilisers for their land and they cannot afford to pay the cost of freight by road. They are cut off and disheartened. They know very well that a pier *ought* to be built if any progress is ever to be made in their community. They see the years pass, themselves growing older, their sons leaving for the Army, the Air Force or the London Police and their daughters getting jobs in Glasgow, they see the land in Glenelg going steadily back, the bracken spreading far up the hillsides above their homes, and the sheep for which they still owe money to the Department of Agriculture declining in quality and numbers—they see all this, but they never see a pier which might enable them to make ends meet. The estimated cost of building a pier at Glenelg is about £4,000, and the local people would find some of the money if the steamship company and the Government would find the rest.

The problems of Scotland are many and diverse, but they nearly all come to this: ' We have a need (it may be for more and better food, more and better houses, better communications), we have men, materials and money in Scotland to supply that need: have we the will-power?'

III

The extract from one of Keats' letters, which stands at the head of this chapter, is evidence that a hundred years ago the country people of Scotland did not need anyone to teach them how to enjoy themselves. It is just the same to-day, except that now there are more village halls. But the move from a draughty barn to a well-built hall has taken nothing from the fun. The dance goes on.

Another welcome 'event' is the whist-drive, sometimes followed by dancing. The popularity of carpet bowls has been steadily increasing in Scotland since the War. In Dumfriesshire there are 59 clubs. So far it is not being played farther north than Aberdeen-shire, though its vogue is constantly extending. In many villages the clubs meet two or three evenings a week. The game is played on a mat with small size bowls. It is perhaps hardly a sign of the natural gaiety of the Scottish villages, since it is usually played in a grim silence! In a Lowland village with which I am acquainted another popular recreation in the village hall is badminton. Matches against neighbouring clubs are planned months ahead, and talked of for weeks after.

The same village made for itself soon after the War an excellent bowling-green; one of the villagers receives a weekly stipend for keeping it in good condition during the summer. Bowls is a popular game, and on a fine evening men of all ages turn out each with his set of bowls to play spirited contests. Curling is of course still better sport, and the match of a thousand or more a side between North and South, which is played at Carsebreck once a winter when the weather is hard enough, excites the whole country. The South had a sequence of eighteen wins between 1880 and 1914. The three matches since the War have all been won by the North and I know a skip for the South who can tell you why.

At one time football was more often played in Scottish country districts than it is now. Readers of Lockhart's *Life of Scott* will recall the description [1] of the famous match between Selkirk and Yarrow, which lasted from 11 a.m. until the dusk of a December day, and ended in a draw. It is still, however, a popular game in the country, though generally played in the summer—the farm worker cannot leave his work in the winter until after dark. Football of course is Scotland's national sport. To see England beaten at Hampden Park is the spectacle above all others most grateful to the Scot; a spectacle which he is able to witness almost every other year.

The long arm of the Government's Physical Fitness Improvement Scheme has not yet shown its hand in Scotland's countryside, and one may wonder what it will do when it arrives. It might adopt Professor Stapledon's

[1] Reprinted in *The Scots Book*, by Ronald MacDonald Douglas.

happy suggestion and institute primitive-golf ; or taking an arrow out of England's quiver, encourage archery. It might even resurrect a sport that flourished in some parts before the War—the old game of hare-and-hounds, in which the Laird's son and the young game-keeper, or whoever else had the fastest pair of shoes, used to lead their fellow-villagers a course through the hills. This was a good winter's pastime, if now rather old-fashioned, and would be followed by a roaring tea before a roaring fire.

The object of ' recreational ' amenities is to promote happiness. In villages where the people are wide-awake and happy already, there should be no interference by well-meaning busybodies. It would be quite easy to make a series of informal regional inquiries to find out where help of this kind is needed. Once a village hall is in being, indoor recrea-tion (which of course includes active exer-cises like dancing, badminton and boxing, as well as the winter programme of the Boy

Scouts, Girl Guides, Women's Rural Institute etc.) tends to run itself. Two or three local enthusiasts are enough to set the ball rolling, and it will soon be found that six evenings a week are too few for all the purposes for which the hall is wanted.

There is still, however, a great need for some movement which will enrich the lives of the young farm hands in the way that the Women's Rural Institutes have widened the lives of the wives and daughters of the farmers and farm workers. Life for a great many of these young men is still, unfortunately, a very empty affair.

I think myself that the solution will be found in something like the School of National Craftsmanship, suggested in the last chapter. What a man wants to make his life a full one is not so much amusement as a ' purpose ': and the mastery of a craft, outside the run of his ordinary occupations, would supply that purpose. All the more when his mastery of the craft is proved by his success in selling the products of his leisure hours ! If the thing could be organised on a national scale, these young men would have the extra stimulus of being contributors to a revival of Scots craftsmanship, so that patriotism as well as the creative instinct and the pleasure of having turned an honest penny would spur their enthusiasm. It was by enlisting a natural enthusiasm that Lord Baden-Powell made the Boy Scout Movement the success it has been, but for that purpose leaders were required, and leaders will be wanted no less if rural craftsmanship is to be revived in Scotland. So we return to the old truth, that the laird who fails to give the lead to his district, to form a headpiece to the rural structure, to be the hub round which the village can revolve (what metaphor you please, but to do the job he is expected to do, and alone can do), and goes to the towns for his money, his amusements and his interests, is the root cause of the depopulation of the countryside. Until he comes back, or someone else goes and fills his place and does his job, the country will not recover.

The Women's Rural Institutes have been a real blessing to Scotland. This is not the occasion, nor is a man well qualified, to make an assessment of all they have done, but among the subjects in which they have given instruction are Cookery, Dress-making, Needlework, Upholstery, Handicrafts and Country Dancing. The number of Institutes in Scotland (September 1936) was 987, with a total membership of over 50,000.

The popularity of rural drama is highly encouraging. There are now 400 village Dramatic Clubs in Scotland. The interest in singing has unfortunately declined, probably because Scotland has little as yet to sing about. Vigorous youths are not content to chant in chorus the praises of their ancestors. They want an inspiration from their own time, and are waiting for the new Burns to put their feelings into immortal song. A better theme this, than the celebration of an Immortal Memory!

RURAL ADULT EDUCATION

The old Mutual Improvement Associations, of which the first was formed at Rhynie in Aberdeenshire in 1847, were among the earliest attempts at rural Adult Education to be made in the United Kingdom. For many years there existed all over Scotland a large number of these clubs, and even now new clubs are occasionally being started. In Nethy Bridge an Association, formed only three years ago, has already a membership of over 120. The members read papers to each other and hold debates and discussions. Altogether if one includes the Literary and Debating Societies, which are really the same, there are nearly 200 still in existence in Scottish villages.

Since the introduction of the potato, nothing has made so much difference to country life as wireless. The other recreations we have mentioned each appeal to somebody: wireless makes an appeal to all. It used to be one of the troubles of the Highlands that radio reception was interfered with by the mountain barriers, but I am informed that since the erection of the high power station at Burghead, probably 98% of the population are now getting good reception.

There is another rural amenity which would contribute much to the happiness of life in country districts, and that is the eradication of local jealousies and of cliques. These reproduce in miniature the least satisfactory side of Scotland's history, with its inbreeding and back-biting—defects only too natural in a small and more or less self-contained unit such as Scotland was, and as a village community still is. The cure for such defects is found in a breadth of contact and of view, which was given to Scotland by her wisest kings and must be provided for country communities, wherever it may be needed, by leadership of the same kind—that of a man who is first among his equals.

CHAPTER X

A PARLIAMENT IN SCOTLAND

' The Rev. James Barr, M.P., who presided, said that a Parliament in Scotland taking the initiative in economic development could set a real example of what Socialism could do.'

Weekly Scotsman, 1st May, 1937.

EXACTLY SO; and the pleasure you take in the prospect of ' a Parliament in Scotland ' *under present conditions* will correspond with your wish to see in Scotland ' a real example of what Socialism can do '. It would be the old story of a Party-government in Scotland all over again: the ruling Party continually in consultation with the corresponding ' Party ' across the Border, as in 1640 when the Scottish Covenanters having climbed into the saddle threw the reins to their co-religionists in England. And within ten years Scotland lay at the feet of Cromwell.

It is not that sort of Parliament that we want in Scotland, and just so long as Socialism is waiting round the corner to exploit an independent Scotland, so long will every Scot who sees a happier destiny than Socialism in store for his country refuse the blind leadership of Nationalists whose one idea for Scotland—let the consequences be what they may—is that she should be governed by Scotsmen.

It is more important that she should be well governed. Nobody of experience suggests that Scotsmen are incapable of ruling themselves, and of doing it much better than we are at present ruled from Whitehall. A change indeed must be made. What matters is that it should be a change for the better. It is simply untrue to say, as the Nationalists in their impatience have sometimes said, that *any* change from the present system would be an improvement. The first essential is that the people of Scotland should see before them a goal, which will unite them, which will attract them without distinction of class or party, and for which they themselves are prepared whole-heartedly to work. That goal in its simplest terms is that every Scot shall have good food to eat and a good house to live in, and that he shall enjoy spiritual and economic freedom.

Neither Socialists nor Conservatives by themselves can save Scotland, for both are governed by the notion that the primary purpose of any trade or industry is to make a profit. The only dispute between them is how that profit shall be divided. The Conservative wishes to keep it; the Socialist wants to see it go in higher wages and increased taxation. What concerns them both is the money.

There never was any system in the world more conservative and tenacious of its old ideas than Socialism. Let Socialism in one country after another go down before the dynamic of events; elsewhere Socialists will still be talking as though their doctrine were in the first flush of its promising, unsullied youth. The Stewart Kings who reigned in England were not more slow to learn a lesson from current history. We may take it therefore that the Scottish Socialists, though many of them are individually most ardent lovers of Scotland, will continue in practice to put their party and doctrine first, will vote as a party against any Government measures tending to help Scotland, because they are Government measures, and in theory will still prefer the Internationalist ideal to any form of nationalism in their own land. If the Socialists rise above these expectations founded on their recent record, they have a great future in front of them, but they have long since lost the living idealism of Keir Hardie. They have become an institution. Their whole system creaks with pedantry, and though their powers of destruction are still vigorous, their power to give life—which is what Scotland wants—

is fled. The Scots workman who votes Socialist is much more interested in Scotland for Scotland's sake than are his political leaders, and from him much help for Scotland may be forthcoming. But it wants tapping, and party-politics (attempted by the Scottish Nationalists) are not the way to tap it. Much richer possibilities await the man who has strength and imagination to reach that latent patriotism. But to reach it calls for leadership of a higher than political order.

The Conservative mind is more interesting than the Socialist, though not more attractive. It presents rather greater varieties, as befits a party one of whose best tenets has been the efficacy of private enterprise. But the generic characteristic, the sign-manual, of a Conservative is the desire to conserve what he has got. Individually the Conservative may be very generous with his money, but as a political being his goal, whether for the State or for himself, is summed up in the words: ' What I have, I hold.'

There comes a stage in the affairs of most successful men and nations when they can no longer afford to take the same risks as they did at the start of their career: they have too much to lose. Concerned only to defend what they have gained, they neither care nor dare to advance: and as the law of Nature runs that nothing in life can stand still, a man or a nation which has reached this point generally begins to go back. An obvious example is the difference in tactics employed by the British Navy at the battles of Trafalgar and of Jutland. Nelson risked everything against superior odds, and won a sweeping victory. Jellicoe, on the other hand, ' The one man on either side ' (in Mr. Churchill's words) ' who could lose the War in a single afternoon,' was evidently very conscious that he had ' too much to lose '. The same phenomenon can sometimes be seen in Sport. A player or a team with a great reputation, when faced by another of a lower rank, often plays with constraint and timidity, fearing to forfeit the fine record which was originally gained by much more spirited methods.

A business firm, after a long period of cumulative success, will sometimes show a similar lack of enterprise: and the same charge might be brought against conservative institutions and governments in general. They are happy in what they have: their energies (not perhaps so abundant now as formerly) are fully occupied in holding it, and while they are very jealous and even pugnacious in preserving the *status quo*, they have no love for costly adventures of which the issue is doubtful. If they fight at all, it will be like the Spartans of a generation many years after Thermopylae, only when they are in a majority of four to one. All their actions are hampered by the abiding thought that they have a lot to lose: and from any new adventure which is proposed to them they turn away sorrowful, ' because they have great possessions.'

History, present no less than past, bristles

with examples of this defeatist outlook, which appears to be connected in some way with the return of men's faculties upon themselves, like dogs who were sent out after a quarry and have tired of seeking it while apparently in full bodily vigour and capacity. If old age be a cause, it is an old age of the spirit: and what caused the man to grow old before his time? He has reached a goal, but there are fresh worlds to conquer: why should he tire of going forward? Is there a circumference to the range of man's spirit, beyond which he cannot freely operate: just as his body cannot freely breathe beyond a certain altitude in the physical world? This view we are very loth to accept, and there have indeed been sufficient examples to the contrary in Man himself to prove it false. The spirit of man has never yet in this world reached its natural frontier.

Is the cause then prudential—a practical application of the precept γνῶθι σεαυτόν—a recognition by man of what he thinks is the limit to his effective power? Such prudence is commended in generals, who will not advance to attack a province which they cannot hold without endangering their former possessions. If the parallel lies, we should be able clearly to determine the proper limits to our capacities, and thereby much energy would be saved. Perhaps this was what Socrates meant when he told us to know ourselves.

No answer, however, to the question can be true which leaves unsatisfied any important part of mankind: and the answer suggested above is, and will always be, unsatisfying to a large number of young people and of those many who keep their youth until they die. For they know that merely to save one's life or one's reputation is to lose it, and that a defensive kind of life which shuns adventures and leaves the spirit to rust, is not the game at all as it was intended and is a disobedience to divine orders. In this sense they interpret the Parable of the Prodigal Son and the Parable of the Talents. The fear of failure, which is perhaps the principal cause of the 'defensive' frame of mind, is discounted in these parables. It seems that this risk, which to the human mind often appears terrible, is not feared for us by our Creator who loves us: the only fear is that, burdened by trying to keep what we have, we may cease to go forward, and so lose ourselves and our chance of 'living' from a totally unfounded fear that we had 'too much to lose'.

These comments apply to all Conservatives who say that we cannot afford to develop the Highlands agriculturally, because the process could not bring an adequate economic return. Such a development of the Highlands must be made the first aim of policy in Scotland, and Scotland will see that in the long run, if not sooner, it produces a more than adequate return, economically as well as spiritually. We must see that the thing is done because it is an adventure for which our country cries out to us,[1] and if any defeatist from the towns

[1] Such an adventure as the Jews have taken on in Palestine—ploughing the land, building, fighting natural obstacles and often the jealousy of the Arabs.

or elsewhere says that the thing is impossible, he should be shipped off at once to the Isle of Mull with a scythe to cut bracken until he has changed his mind.

What then? If neither Conservatives nor Socialists alone can help us, and if Scottish Nationalism cannot flourish while party politics continue to divide us, what then? The answer is, Unite the nation—not along either of the old party tram-lines which will never meet till, please God, they come to an end— but by making it gradually aware of a faith which it owes, not to a party, but to Scotland above all parties even that of Scottish Nationalism: and let the people realise this faith, not in talk but in their daily lives—some on a humble stage, as better farmers this year than in the year before, each man at his own craft or industry plying his hammer the better for Scotland's sake—and others as vocation calls them, planning together the means by which their fellow-Scots shall live larger and happier lives. Among these means will be an ever increasing freedom from the restraints of Whitehall. There is work enough of all kinds to be done for Scotland and in Scotland, and in the doing of it we may find that unity which we have lost since 1513—a unity which will not only much assist the work itself, but will win for us our freedom.

The English are one of the most reasonable people who ever lived, and are always ready to make concessions to anyone both resolute and friendly, especially when some practical advantage is to follow the concession. There is no manner of doubt that if Scotland were *united* in asking for a large degree of governmental freedom, she would receive it—the overriding questions of taxation and foreign policy being still determined by the common Parliament at Westminster. It would be a great practical advantage to England to have as her neighbour a prosperous and deeply contented Scotland.

The present system is open to two immediate objections. The Scottish Office in Whitehall, with branches shortly to be concentrated in the new Government buildings on Calton Hill, is ultimately responsible for Scottish Agriculture, Fisheries, Health, Education and Scottish affairs generally. This is too much work for one small Department, and it is not surprising that complaints of delay are many and bitter.

The second objection is that to which Mr. Henderson Stewart, M.P., referred recently in a letter to Mr. Elliot. The Westminster Parliament has not time enough in these days to give adequate attention to Scottish problems; it appears that during the last three Parliaments less than 16 hours per year on the average have been given to debates on Scottish Estimates. This means that important decisions are being taken, and a great deal of money is being spent, at the instance of officials without proper opportunity of control by the representatives of the Scottish people. That is wrong in theory, for it is a

travesty of the democratic system whose
benefits we are supposed to be enjoying; but
it is still worse in practice, for it means that
the officials are being allowed to govern
Scotland according to their own ideas. Under
official rule one may get the worst of both
worlds, the red tape of Socialist pedantry and
the impotent hand-wringing of Conservatives
who have reached the unshakeable conviction
that ' nothing can be done '. The officials
are the more likely to have their way since
between them and the people lies the buffer-
state of ambitious politicians, men whose success in the eyes of those who can promote
them to higher office will be judged in part
by their ability to stifle criticism. On the
other hand, officials are often impeded in
their administrative work by having to prepare answers to irresponsible questions.

The new Government buildings on Calton
Hill are not therefore in themselves a guarantee that Scotland will be governed any differently than she has been in the recent past.

THE VETERINARY SERVICES

What concerns us is not the shell of the walnut, but its kernel. How far are the Scottish people being allowed control over their own affairs?

A significant case occurred this summer. The Minister of Agriculture with the consent of the Scottish Office decided to centralise in Whitehall the control of Scotland's veterinary services, which have up to now been managed from Edinburgh and are acknowledged to be at present better than the corresponding services in England. This decision was justified by the Under-Secretary of State for Scotland, speaking in the House of Commons on 29th June as follows: ' Let the Committee remember that Scotland is an exporter of cattle to England. It is very important that the exports of Scottish farmers should not be interfered with, and if you are to have separate centres it might involve the closing of Scottish cattle to England. It is to our advantage to have a centralised system.' We should also remember that Scotland is a great exporter of human

227

beings into England, and by the same argument the Minister of Health (if he wished) could justify the centralisation of Scottish health services in Whitehall.

The time will come, perhaps before very long, when this process of rocking the baby to sleep with soothing promises which at the same moment are being broken at the other end of the nursery, will have to stop. Self-government as such has no great appeal to the Scottish (or indeed the English) people, or the percentage of voters at elections would be much higher than it is. What we demand is that Scotland shall be governed with an eye to the well-being of the people of Scotland, and not merely as part of Great Britain. If this condition were satisfied, the process might be carried out in London and the Scottish people would raise no objection.

The Scottish Nationalists attach, in my view, too great an importance to legislative machinery. Legislative machinery alone will do no good to a people that is not prepared to heal itself. There are now signs, however, that Scotland is once more in the mood to heal herself, and it would therefore pay our rulers to see that the machinery which exists *shall be made to work*. The machinery needs improving and modernising, no doubt, but above all it needs using. The decision not to enforce, and later not to adapt to modern conditions, the Sea Fisheries Regulation Act (Scotland) of 1895 has been mentioned. Because the Scottish fishermen, it may be presumed, do not command enough votes, the Government machinery has not been operated to save them—although they patrolled our coasts, swept up mines, sank U-boats and maintained a fish-supply in the last War, and will do so again if need arise, so far as they are able. The Nationalists are well justified in claiming that a Scottish Government would equip these fishermen to hold their own upon the seas.

One cannot see over the horizon. If in present circumstances Scotland were to obtain the self-government for which she has not yet asked, the parties sending members to the first Scottish Parliament would no doubt be principally those with which we are familiar at Westminster and I have given reasons earlier in this chapter for my view that neither Conservatives nor Socialists are likely to assist in building the Scotland of our dreams. To the question therefore whether at this stage a Parliament in Scotland is to be desired I would answer No, with the reservation that circumstances may so change that in the life-time of our sons a large degree of self-government for Scotland might become highly desirable. A common system of taxation and identity of foreign policy for England and Scotland will always be essential.

That which would hasten self-government for Scotland most surely would be a continued disposition on the part of Westminster and Whitehall to think that Scottish problems can safely be neglected. The Scottish people are waking up at last and will not be satisfied any longer by an external façade, by speeches, by Calton Hill buildings, by assurances that Scotland rules the Empire and so forth. What will satisfy us will be to see our fishing-boats reconditioned, small-holders under the Department of Agriculture living in security, communications with the West of Scotland brought up to date by the provision of faster services and piers where needed: these as a first instalment of good government of Scotland for the Scots.

Such measures have been long overdue. They would be carried out by a Scottish Government: they can be carried out by a British Government at Westminster. If they are not, the conclusion will be plain—that so far as these things are concerned, we should be better to govern ourselves. And there are many such things.

Until quite recently the ruling classes in Scotland used to laugh at the mere idea of self-government. With reason they are less sure now. It depends on how we are governed from Westminster during the next few years; the verdict will lie with the Scottish people.

The theoretical objections to self-government for Scotland would be largely removed if taxation and foreign policy were still decided by the common Parliament at Westminster. The Nationalists will never overcome the strong prejudice against self-government unless they make these two reasonable concessions.

They suffer from two further handicaps. Their Party does not at present contain a single statesman whom the Scottish people would be prepared to trust with a Government, and they lack conspicuously that touch of broad-minded greatness which Scotland herself needs for her flowering.

The charge of narrowness is often brought against the Nationalists, who answer by pointing to the four Objects of their policy (see page 235). There it is proposed to defend the Empire by consultation on an equal foot-

ing with England; but when the question
arises of defending the Empire by contribu-
tions, there is no longer any talk of an equal
footing. In a pamphlet entitled *Self-Government in Practice* (The Scottish National Party:
6d.) it is proposed that Scotland's payments
towards Imperial Defence should be based on
the same principle as those of Northern
Ireland and the Isle of Man, namely, her
capacity to pay—the rate to be determined
by a joint commission (as it is in Ulster) consisting of Scottish and English Treasury representatives. In 1931, the last year for which
figures were then available, Scotland's contribution to Imperial purposes was £25,000,000,
i.e. £5 4 0 per head. England's contribution
was over £10 per head, but the Nationalists do
not emphasize that England on account of her
greater wealth has shouldered a heavier share
of the cost. They keep their eyes fixed rather
on the lightness of the burdens borne by
Ulster (5/- per head) and the Isle of Man
(£1 5 0). We are offered the glittering

prospect that, if we were assessed on the same basis as the Isle of Man, we should pay £6,000,000; if on the same basis as Ulster, £1,000,000. Thus ' a sum of from 19 to 24 millions a year would be set free to relieve taxation, to help industry, agriculture or fishing, or to set on foot works of public utility.'[1] If in the meantime our Imperial defences were breached, these putative millions would vanish overnight, and the only thing left for the Nationalists to divide would be the blame.

According to the latest Treasury Return, for 1934-35, Scotland's contribution to Imperial expenditure fell temporarily to £19,446,000, and that of England and Wales to £372,549,000. It is interesting to note also in the same Return, that Scotland contributes 8.63% of the total Revenue collected from England, Wales and Scotland, and that of the sum allocated to Local Expenditure in the three countries, Scotland receives 12.39%.

[1] *Self-Government in Practice*, p. 28.

THE SCOTTISH NATIONALISTS

The Objects of the Scottish National Party are as follows:

(1) *There shall be established in Scotland a Parliament which shall be the final authority on all Scottish affairs, including Taxation and Finance.*

(2) *Scotland shall share with England the rights and responsibilities they as Mother Nations have jointly created and incurred within the British Empire.*

(3) *Machinery shall be set up whereby Scotland with the other British Nations shall deal jointly with such responsibilities and in particular with such matters as Defence, Foreign Policy and Customs.*

(4) *The Scottish National Party shall be independent of all other political parties.*

It is difficult to judge from this Programme what would happen if the Scottish Nationalists ever came to power. Would Tariff barriers, for example, be a necessary consequence of Object No. 1? That the Nationalists hope not, is a fair deduction from the wording of Object No. 3, which would set up machinery to settle, jointly with England and the other British Nations, *such matters as . . . Customs.* Take whisky, a Scottish product. Suppose the Scottish Parliament decided to remove the present excise duty of over 8/- per bottle on whisky, and the English Chancellor of the Exchequer, as is probable, wished to retain it. The price of whisky would be 4/6 or less per bottle in Scotland and 12/6 in England. In order to collect his 8/-, the English Chancellor would be compelled either to set up customs at Carlisle and Newcastle (and keep a watch all along the coast for small boats at night) or use his influence to induce the Scots Parliament to restore the whisky duty. That the English, if they wished, could have their way in such a struggle is only too obvious, though I do not doubt that there are Nationalists who would dispute it: Scotland's heavy industries, the main source of the taxable wealth of our country, depend to a large extent on England's goodwill. The Nationalists believe that a spirit of give-and-take would smooth out any difficulties, and their plans include a Customs Union for this purpose. How exactly this would work, the Nationalists have not said because they do not know; but one must expect that in practice Scotland's fiscal autonomy would be severely limited. For many reasons it would surely be wise to abandon altogether the idea of raising taxation differently in the two countries.

Whatever criticisms may be brought against the Scottish Nationalists in one detail or another, it behoves us to thank them for having stirred up Scotland. That is the first great service they are doing, and the second is their research work in other countries from which Scotland has lessons to learn. Denmark, the Faroes, Ireland, Germany, have all something to teach us. The Faroe Islanders in common with the people of Orkney,[1] have

---

[1] Kirkwall, the capital of the Orkneys, celebrated last July the eight hundredth anniversary of the founding of St. Magnus Cathedral. Mr. James Fergusson, who is not a Nationalist, describing this event in the *Spectator* wrote as follows: ' This great and memorable festival was carried out in a burgh whose population,

developed their agriculture and the general standard of life far above what has been attained in the Highlands. The Danes also. In a recent issue of *Time and Tide*, Eric Linklater reported the opinion of a Danish agricultural expert, Mr. Arne Ström:

' If I had known more about Scotland when I was a young man, I wouldn't have gone to America. I would have come to the Highlands. I would have brought with me a hundred Danes and we would have formed a colony. And we would have made a great success.' This was said after a walk on foot through the Western Isles of Scotland; Mr. Ström ' knew that Denmark, a little country, much of it dunes and peat-moss, had achieved agricultural prosperity in face of all diffi-

---

3,500, is not much more than that of a good-sized English village. We knew before that the people of Orkney were hospitable, industrious, prosperous and contented. We know something more about them now; that they have a lively appreciation of their history and traditions, a spirit of dignity worthy of their great past, an artistic fertility out of all proportion to their numbers, and a welcome incapacity to conceive that inferiority has any relation to size. Scotland has something to learn from Orkney.'

culties by concerted effort and the use of modern knowledge. He saw that great areas of Scotland, far richer by nature, were inhabited only by a few black-faced sheep and some Old Age pensioners. He was not merely horrified, but, having been a farmer himself, jealous of the opportunities that the waste land offered.'

The usual reaction in Scotland to this sort of depreciatory comparison with a small and relatively unimportant country has been one of indifference. The Scottish Nationalists, by contrast, go to Scandinavia and study Scandinavian methods at first hand. Sir Alexander MacEwen for example has been in Denmark recently, collecting information about Folk High Schools for rural districts.[1] For all this

[1] Folk High Schools have been a feature of Danish life for over seventy years. They give education to men and women between the ages of 18 and 25, and are intended to fit rural workers for a full life; the three cardinal subjects taught in the Folk High Schools are History, Danish and Song. Adult Education in Scotland seems more likely to follow the lines of the Village Colleges established at Sawston and elsewhere by the Cambridgeshire Education Committee.

exploratory work much praise is due, but it may not be impertinent to end on a note of warning and of wider hope.

First and last, small-mindedness is the vice against which Scotland in rediscovering herself must chiefly guard. To borrow good ideas from Denmark and the Faroe Islands is one thing: to be content, as some individual Nationalists would like us to be content, with the same influence that Denmark at present exerts upon the world, is quite another. We must do greater things than these; clearly the British Empire lies in the centre of balance and must either rock the world into disaster or lead it into new life. Freely we have received from the world, freely we must give, and our gift to it in the coming years must be spiritual leadership. But just as the leadership of the world is with the Empire, so the leadership of the Empire is with the Mother Countries. This is the fact to-day. In fifty years' time the Empire may perhaps pivot round Canada, as some who know that great

Dominion predict. By then the political crisis will have passed: for good or ill, Germany, Russia, Italy, Spain, Japan will have settled down on their course. The economic system, invented in Britain and not more than 150 years old, which makes profit the mainspring of human activities even at the cost of a healthy, happy life—that economic system may have given way to a better one.

Our chance of leadership therefore is not fifty years ahead, but now. We have before us a task well worthy of our gifts—one for which, Sir John Orr has told us, Scotland as the home of democracy is peculiarly suited. That task is to show that an independent people, retaining liberty of thought and speech, can live together like brothers—a family of which every member is well fed and housed, and as many as possible are living as their own masters on the land.

Such a family—strong, self-reliant, and helping one another—would be in effect the best Parliament that Scotland has ever had.

CHAPTER XI

CLEARING THE GROUND

'It is the future that matters. The past is only a make-believe for those who have no future to look forward to.'

ELIZABETH S. HALDANE

I HAD the good fortune in 1933 to publish for Miss Haldane her book on our country in the nineteenth century, *The Scotland of Our Fathers*. The success of that book showed, among other things, the interest which Scots people take in the history of their past. Many a smile we raise upon English lips by our constant reminding them of Bannockburn, as though in a record of unbroken misfortunes that was our one bright day. There were other such days, both by land and sea, as a better acquaintance with Scots history would inform us, and if it

242

is true that Scotland—like Germany—suffers from a sense of inferiority, recourse to the history books would be our best cure. There is excellent material now available for study, and it is well that we should know the rock from whence we are hewn.

But how deep does our interest in the subject go? A Scots mother was talking to me recently about her children's education and she said, ' Scottish history—I should call it interesting, but not important.' She was wrong, for though what matters is the future, and for a Scottish mother the future of Scotland most of all, yet how shall we avoid the mistakes of the past unless we have studied the past? And how shall we win a new Bannockburn in our sons' life-time without first knowing by what steps Scotland was led and tutored up to the old one? It is an error to think that these great events in history just ' happened '. They were cared for, planned and worked for through long years by men and women not very different inwardly from ourselves—by our forefathers, at any rate, and we must have inherited some of their tenacity and some of their gifts. No, for a Scot who has a mind to re-pay the debt he owes to his country, Scottish history is a long way more than interesting. He must master its essentials, until he knows how to apply some of its lessons: chief among these will be the lesson that only when she has been united, has Scotland been secure and happy—and since James IV fell at Flodden, she has never been united.

There is a great chance here for Scottish schools to handle History in a really practical way. Will they take it?

It lies with the young minds of Scotland to-day to settle this question, whether Scotland shall have a future to look forward to. Cushioned about by the seas, and propped against the comfortable pillow of England, Scotland has for a long time been dozing. Of Jairus' daughter it could be said, 'the maid is not dead, but sleepeth.' Of Scotland the converse may soon be true.

LAYING THE FOUNDATIONS

Assume a young Scot, eager and devoted to his country, reading these words: ' It lies with the young minds of Scotland to-day to settle . . . ' He might ask, ' What can I settle and how? By mere wishing?' And the answer is, ' Instead, by sheer willing.' There must come the fibre of resolution; and where two or three and then more, are gathered together, the foundations will be laid. The technical difficulties will yield quickly to research: this may seem glib optimism, but the line of advance is marked out in another chapter of this book by Sir John Orr, whose authority will not be questioned. Greater than any of the technical difficulties, is the lack of faith and perseverance to surmount them. Because of this the destiny of Scotland is given into our hands, to revive or to lose. In our decision lies the country for which so many great men have died: shall not we for Scotland's sake, at last stand up and live?

Throughout this book, this idea of a full life will be found recurring at every stage and in many various forms. It must be the key-note and the mainspring of the new Scotland which we shall leave to our sons.

II

From the Scotland of our sons we should wish to exclude all the bitterness of division which marked the Scotland of our grand-fathers. In a Scotland eager to stand once more on its own feet, the most natural bitter-ness is against the Irish. Statistics of emi-grants from the Irish Free State are only com-piled in respect of those going to countries which are neither in Europe nor bordering on the Mediterranean Sea. The number of these during the past five years was as follows:

EMIGRANTS

	Irish Free State and British	Aliens	Total
1932	- - 811	60	871
1933	- - 903	72	975
1934	- - 1,034	144	1,178
1935	- - 1,031	107	1,138
1936	- - 1,261	101	1,362

Particulars of total passenger movement (including Migrants) by sea during the same period were as follows:

	From Irish Free State	To Irish Free State
1932	- - 399,133	405,648
1933	- - 376,586	373,973
1934	- - 412,473	401,471
1935	- - 448,465	434,120
1936	- - 502,568	481,029

In 1932, when the depression in Great Britain was still severe, several thousand more people entered the Irish Free State by sea than left. In the four following years, during which trade continuously improved in Great Britain, the trend was rapidly reversed, until in 1936 21,539 more people sailed out of the Free State than sailed into it. Only 1,362 of this total emigrated outside Europe and the Mediterranean, leaving a balance of 20,177 who left the I.F.S. by boat and did not return. A few went to fight in Spain, and a few others may have settled elsewhere in Europe, but the vast majority came over by the boat to Glasgow, Liverpool and Bristol, and are still with us. Besides these, there are the immigrants from Northern Ireland, whose numbers can only be guessed. It is believed in Glasgow that actually more Roman Catholics come to Scotland from Ulster, where they are in a minority, than from the I.F.S.

There are three reasons why this Irish invasion is resented in Scotland. The least important is that Irish names appear regularly in the law-courts. It is pleaded that this is the natural result of a manly type being forced to live in the conditions of a Glasgow slum. Some crimes of which the Irish in Glasgow have been convicted do not suggest manliness. Certainly the conditions in which many of these people live make a decent life almost impossible; the point is that the conditions themselves are made worse by this flow of Irish, which it would be highly desirable—in the interests no less of the Irish than of Scotland—to check.

Secondly, there is the fear of Catholicism. The Irish from the Free State are Catholics, and because they breed much faster than the Protestants do, Catholicism is on the rise. That is a menace which the average Scot holds in traditional dread. To reply, as the Catholics do, that we ought to welcome their faith as the one sure bulwark against atheism, is really no answer. Scotland does not welcome it; some of the reasons go far back into history, but one quite up-to-date and simple one is that the Catholics are thought to be taking all they can from Scotland and putting much less into it. They send many Irish children to be educated at the public expense in Scotland, they make conspicuous use of public hospitals—and their donations are nearly always made to Catholic hospitals or other Catholic institutions.

Lastly, the Irish are content to do rougher and more menial work than the Scots. The best navvies in Britain are Irish. Many tunnels, sewers, etc., in Scotland are the work of poorly-paid Irish labourers, and we ought to be grateful to them for what they have done.

Nevertheless Scotland is severely hit by unemployment, and will be very much more so
when rearmament slows down. It follows
that the extra Irish labourers who come to
Scotland from now onwards mean either so
many Scots workers out of a job, or alter-
natively so many more Irish on the Scottish
dole.

Up to 1931 Great Britain was willing to be
the dumping-ground for the world's goods,
and it seemed unthinkable that we should
ever change that policy. It seems to-day unthinkable that we should ever place any
restrictions upon Irish immigrants into Great
Britain, if only because Ulster is a part of the
United Kingdom. The Irish Free State limits
the right to apply for unemployment assistance
(as distinct of course from the benefits of Unemployment Insurance) to persons either of
Free State nationality or who for the five preceding years have ordinarily resided in the
I. F. S. Ideally our right policy is to place
Scotland so firmly on her feet that she will not

only breed freely from her own stock, but will welcome settlers from overseas. But we have to set our own house in order first.

Some form of restriction upon new Irish coming in to Scotland would be a psychological advantage, quite apart from its direct effect upon our figures of employment. For you cannot begin with any confidence to restore a broken building if the sea is at all times pouring into its foundations, and you cannot help Scotland to recover her poise and balance if she is to be subject, at every time of rising prosperity, to a fresh invasion of aliens or semi-aliens from over the water.

It must, however, be clearly recognised that the Irish who are already established here are not aliens, nor to be treated as such. Their children, if not themselves, will be Scottish-born, and will be woven into the stuff of Scotland's life. For an experimental period we should deal with the Irish as Hamlet wished to deal with wedlock: ' I say,' (he said) ' we will have no more marriages:

those that are married already, all but one,
shall live; the rest shall keep as they are.'

III

Let us remember throughout our policy
that what we are aiming at is a better Scotland
for the next generation, and that our sense of
this word ' better ' will include not only the
material benefits which have occupied almost
the whole attention of statesmen in the last
half-century, but also the spiritual ones which
are just as necessary now as they were in
simpler times when they were more easy to
distinguish and appreciate.

The first obstacle to be removed is the belief, so natural to a democracy under universal
franchise in an age of immense material
advance, that life is to be reckoned solely or
chiefly according to material standards. This
belief is taking firm root in British public life.
Politicians rest their appeal to voters on that
basis: they do not think we would respond to
a higher class of appeal, and besides, they

would by now be really shy—almost ashamed
—of addressing us in any language except that
which is intelligible to our pockets. To talk
publicly of spiritual values as though they had
any longer any power or influence in our
enlightened days, has become unfashionable;
those of our leaders who still hold such a
belief, do not expect to ' get it across ' to the
people.¹   In its place, a new form of secular
religion has sprung up: it is a compromise
between the new materialist philosophy and
the Second Commandment of Christ, ' Thou
shalt love thy neighbour as thyself.

The natural result of this semi-religious
leadership has been that people have come
less and less to believe in God: the outward
forms are satisfied by a loudly expressed belief
in something resembling one of His own
commandments, for whose performance there

¹ Mr. Baldwin, half Scots by birth, was an exception.   So are the
present leaders, both Scots, of the National Churches: the Moder-
ator of the Church of Scotland brought home to the Assembly the
harsh plight of the Highlands; the Archbishop of Canterbury
brought home to us all the spiritual meaning of the Coronation.
But these men *are* exceptions.

is a cash compensation in this world, so that if the specifically ' religious ' side of the belief should prove illusory, nevertheless the investment will repay and justify itself in seats for politicians, continued benefices for the clergy, security and good order for the middle classes, improved conditions for the poor, and for shallow good-hearted people everywhere the ' comfy ' feeling often voiced by hostesses at Charity Balls. The basis of the whole thing, *by itself*—that is, when not enshrined in the true religion expressed in Christ's first and great commandment—is essentially material; and as such it has no living, driving force. It fails completely to satisfy. It masquerades as a religion, and is bogus, but like any other religion it has become institutionalised, and has many vested interests dependent upon it. Therefore to challenge its claims to our worship is dangerous and is, in fact, not done. This is the first thing we must do. This idol, alien in origin but now threatening to invade Scotland, must be broken, and taken away.

THE COURAGE TO THINK

The following paragraph, reproduced by permission from *Life and Work*, may serve as a pointer to the future.

> In the next place, God's will is that you should be courageous enough to think yourself out. I call to mind the saying of a famous professor of mine in the University of Glasgow. Through the haze of memory I can still see that beautiful face of his, lit up by two blazing, grey eyes, and hear a voice, aflame with urgency and conviction, crying his prophet's cry, 'Believe me, gentlemen, there is but one tragedy in this universe and one only, one that is fatal to all growth, one that is final and irrecoverable, and this is the tragedy of the man or woman who refuses to think.' His voice died away into a note of solemnity that seemed to make that winter's morning more sombre and desolate than ever before, and through the dark we watched the ghosts of men and women whose misery was complete. They were the faces of spirits who had refused to think.[1]

IV

The next superstition which must be destroyed is similar to the first, and is derived from it. It is the prestige of the towns as against the country. So long as things material

[1] Rev. Alistair Maclean, B.D., Daviot (*Life and Work*, Jan. 1937).

were our standard, obviously the prosperous, sky-scraping towns, full of shops and cinemas and bustle of affairs, would take applause from the humble steading and Nature's own quiet equipment of life and beauty, and it was forgotten or disregarded that just as the tree draws sustenance from the earth in which it has its roots, so the towns derive not only their food but their importance from the countryside. Consequently, it has been assumed that the towns are alive and what matters, and that the country is dead and doesn't. This idea is reinforced by the preponderant voting strength of the industrial population, and so gradually the nation tends to become more and more urban-minded. People leave the countryside, attracted by the hope of better pay and more amusements in the towns, and as the countryside becomes depopulated, so the voting power of the towns becomes proportionately still greater, and the process accelerates.

The teachers, if they wished, could play a

great part in arresting that process. But do they want to arrest it? Are they not, of all classes in Britain, the most subject to this superstition that in the towns you will find a better life than in the country? If the teachers as a whole could be set this question, they would almost certainly refer you to the economics of it, and it remains, of course, true that until you can guarantee to workers on the land a market, a profitable market, for their products—the land is likely to continue as Cordelia, the neglected daughter to whom her deluded father will turn only when the towns have let him down. That this will eventually happen is quite certain. How much wiser we should be to frame a country-mind in our people now when we can do it naturally and gradually, than to do it at the last moment under the spur of mass-starvation when it will be too late to acquire the country habit of mind.

The big fear at present is war: we may slide past that, but on a long view our export trade cannot recover its pre-eminence which gave Britain her wealth; and all the time we are taxing away the supports. When the last millionaire has died and the last big estate is broken up, how are we going to feed a million or two millions of our people doing nothing, besides the five or six millions who by that time will have qualified for an Old Age Pension? It is not undue pessimism to look forward to a time when the towns and the teachers will be unable to solve a problem which the towns and the teachers are now merrily piling up. May we not ask the school-masters of Scotland to look ahead and to weigh this problem as carefully as they would the provision of food for their children? They know already the difficulty of finding jobs for the younger generation: they wear out their brains in training pupils for an indus-trial world which does not need them, when all the time the land *does* need them.

A love of the land can only be engrained in tender years. That is why our people are leaving the land. They are kept at school to any age, which causes them, when they leave, to be afraid of a cow and to think that it is a dirty animal. They want a black-coated job, or something indoors to sit at a desk, as they have sat in school. . . . All the measures of the Ministry of Agriculture to get people back to the land are an idle tale unless the love of the land and the knowledge of what it can do is created by a practical working knowledge at a very tender age.

A doctor in Orkney told me, when I was there nearly 30 years ago, that one of the causes of the growing prosperity of the Orkney people was the practice of having little boys of tender years acting as herd boys in the summer months. There are no fences there, and these boys' services were essential. They resided with the employers, and were treated as members of their families. On their return to school in autumn their physique and mentality were so improved that though they had had a shorter period at school than the boys of those parents who thought it beneath them to let their sons be so employed, they easily outstripped them in scholastic achievement. They were expert farmers by the time they were 15, and knowing what the land could do for them they sought to get a piece in Orkney, or went to Orkney friends in Canada, Australia, or New Zealand, where, being practically useful, they immediately found employment, and soon afterwards started as farmers on their own account.[1]

[1] From a letter to *The Times*, 22nd June, 1937, by Mr. F. A. Macquisten, M.P. for Argyllshire.

CLEARING THE GROUND

It is good to hear that the Airlie Training Centre, opened in 1936 by the Angus Rural Community Council for the training of unemployed boys in agriculture and forestry, is proving a big success. The Centre is full, and employment is found for the boys when their training is completed. This is the way to keep Scots boys on the land and to keep them happy, and it is to be hoped that the example will be widely followed.

Concerned by the lack of trained woodmen, the Royal English Forestry Society recently sent to the Forestry Commission a recommendation that two training schools for foresters should be founded in England, and the Commission has decided to start a short experimental course on approved private estates under approved instructors.

If economics would approve a more equal balance between town and country, so also would the non-material needs of the nation. This phrase is the title of a chapter in Professor R. G. Stapledon's new book, *The Hill*

Lands of Britain. It is a book which every Scotsman ought to read. He concludes this chapter with the following paragraph:

> It is for these reasons that we as a nation, and before it is too late, must in some measure and by some means seek out the land, and associate with the enterprise and affairs of the land, and if to organize this we have to take great risks, still so urgent is the need that these great risks must be taken. Let us only be as thoughtful, as scientific and as farseeing as we possibly can be in laying our plans. Let us also courageously face the necessary cost. A century ago the country was behind the Government which put up 20 millions to compensate slave-owners. That meant far more in those days than the sums which would now be necessary to free the people of our own country from the influences of a spurious civilization and of a corroding environment.

Profoundly right as he is, where—short of a national calamity—is the lever by which he will move the vast urban population to agree with him? He is not likely to win his fight in Britain as a whole. It is in Scotland, if anywhere, that his dream will come true, partly because the Highlands are crying out for just such an improvement of rough pasture as in all his books he recommends, but chiefly because upon this problem of adjusting the balance between town and country hangs the whole future of Scotland, and her sons and daughters will not lightly see that vanish into nothing.

A good deal of the problem depends on *the women*—and the fact is rarely recognised. The Scots idea of marriage is like the French—a working partnership, with life in common, not in parallel sections: the wife expects to pull her weight in what her man is doing. And in the Highlands at least there is the old Celtic tradition—Norse, too—of respect for women, at least for those who stay on one side of a definite line. So the women are a force. ' On a farm ' (say the Danes) ' the woman is everything. She makes it.' And country life falls harder, in proportion, upon her. A house uses a lot of water in a day: water is heavy, and to carry it from the burn, and peats to heat it, in wet weather

262

or snow, makes one appreciate the idea of taps!

Then again there is the question of prestige. The town has been given it. The country has an inferiority-complex, instilled by the teachers and by social habit. Because of this the women want to put their sons in starched-collar jobs. And the girls want high heels and silk stockings. That sense of inferiority is one of the major problems; and the women are crucial again. Every woman wants her man to *score*, to succeed, win the fight. That's basic human nature, and very sound, too. But if she has a wrong idea of what success is, that may be even worse than if they both have. It is an end to peace for him, probably, or else she has a grievance. Imagine a woman with a grievance, in a bare Highland glen like Glencoe! There is a lot of both melancholia and religious mania about the Highlands, more in women than in men.

This, of course, is to paint the picture at its worst. But it shows how a recovered prestige, the knowledge that they are putting as much into the common stock as the towns, would have a real influence in keeping country people and their children on the land. The false prestige of the towns has to be smashed before Scotland can effectively begin, in the language of the race-course, to ' sit down and ride '.

V

The third idea which for that purpose Time must dispel is the prestige of England as against Scotland. So much prejudice has been aroused on this question, and so many misconceptions about it are rampant on both sides of the Border—not that the English are inclined to take the matter seriously—that a Scot who is at all concerned for his country must make up his mind clearly what he wants, before he can begin to be understood or to initiate any decisive action.

It is widely, but vaguely, supposed that Scotland's material well-being not only depends—as indeed it does—on our keeping on our present excellent terms with England, but also requires that we shall remain in permanent tutelage—a province, no more. Until spiritual forces are allowed to resume their proper part in life, few people—whether Scots or English—can see any objection to Scotland remaining what she is, a province, and no longer a kingdom. If it were true that this condition were essential to her present level of well-being, there would be an end of all argument on the question, since a voluntary lowering of the standard of living in pursuit of what can be represented as a sentimental object, could never be successfully recommended to the people of Scotland. It would not be desirable if it could. Don Quixote is dead.

But the supposed contrast between Scotland's material prosperity and the fullness of her national life is unreal. It is possible for her to have both; indeed, the two will interact to each other's strengthening, as is right and natural, in place of the artificial and deadening separation from which both now suffer.

In what way, then, does the prestige of England overshadow us to our detriment? Only in this, that many Scots have ceased to think of Scotland as an individual Kingdom and Nation any more; and whereas some might regard this as of no account, it does in a thousand ways rob Scotland of the strength and the service that she needs from her sons.

To evoke this service to the full, Scotland needs to be re-established in the minds of her people. We have to find in our immediate future history an inspiration as strong as we draw from our past. We have lived on the spiritual reservoirs laid up by Wallace and Bruce, the Fourth James, Mary Stewart, Montrose, Claverhouse, Prince Charles and the rest of them, and those reservoirs are beginning to run dry. It is our task to open up in Scotland new wells of inspiration for the Scots.

CHAPTER XII

LAND AND PEOPLE: THE NEW INSPIRATION

' The Scotland that God loves is the people.'

IVERACH M^CDONALD

BEFORE SCOTLAND can be herself once more, her sons have three things to do. They must regain touch with a living God: they must regain touch with the land; and they must love Scotland with that single-hearted devotion which has been called the chastity of the soul.

This book is concerned largely with the land. We must regain touch with the land for a hundred reasons that lie too deep in our blood for the mind to understand, but there are other reasons that the mind can understand, and among them is our national spirit of independence, which can be sustained only by an intimate connection with the soil from which we draw our food. Town life is fundamentally insecure, as a war would too plainly show: the sense of insecurity is one of the great evils of our time, and a return of some considerable part of the population to the land would alleviate that sense of insecurity both in townsmen and countryfolk alike.

The love of Scotland has always been intimately linked with the love of God and the love of the countryside. The three are one right through our history, as they must be one also in our hearts. That is the groundwork of this book, whose purpose is to show (in outline rather than in detail) how Scotland can become herself again.

II

' If Alexander had one ambition ', writes Mr. Fergusson of the King who ruled Scotland in her Golden Age,[1] ' it was to see his people

---

[1] ALEXANDER THE THIRD, by James Fergusson.

independent. As a young man he freed them
from the threatened domination of the King
of Norway. In his middle life he supported
the Scottish Church in its struggles for independence of Rome.' And he prepared Scotland for the long war in which she preserved
her freedom against the challenge of England.
This was a noble ambition for a King to wear
in his heart, and he fulfilled it.

Seeing also we have acknowledged that
Scotland, if she is to become her true self
once more, must recover touch with God, it
would be only fitting to ask what was the
ambition of Christ on earth. His answer
was this: 'I am come that they might
have life, and that they might have it more
abundantly.'

These two ambitions, of our earthly and
our spiritual King, are more than compatible:
the one implies the other. For unless a
nation is in some sense independent, it cannot have an abundant life: and that is true also
of a man. What the degree of independence

should be, is a question which every age will answer differently. Christ encouraged the Jews to go on paying tribute to Caesar, and told them that this was not a very important question: yet He wept as He foresaw the capture and destruction of Jerusalem.

What matters, He might say, is that a nation should enjoy enough political independence to enable it to keep the channels of its spiritual life running clear and full: and enough material independence also, for though ' a man's life *consisteth* *not* in the abundance of the things which he possesseth ', yet a sufficiency he must have if the spiritual life is not to be dwarfed too. Victorian cant sometimes said that only morals mattered, and Georgian cant sometimes says that only the physical needs matter. Morals indeed in the ultimate sense only matter so far as they reflect the spiritual life within and re-act on that of others. But the spiritual life and the physical life both matter together, while they are together: as Blake says (through the mouth of a friendly Devil), 'Man has no Body distinct from his Soul.'

Of course Christ, when He said that He had come to give His people a full life, meant very much more than political freedom on the one hand and material prosperity on the other. Both these in their degree are the necessary conditions of that full life, but if we go on to ask what more we want for our countrymen and ourselves, we come quickly into the stuff of which great literature is made. The deep longings of the heart are known to all of us, with that which arouses them—love, friendship, Nature's beauty or grimness, great music, the huge inexplicable tragedy of life and its still vaster hope, the will to fulfilment and the will to service, merging together until the original instinct of self-preservation is lost in the desire of self-sacrifice for some Being which includes and yet far exceeds our own selves: these are things which men feel on a mountain-top at evening and elsewhere as the spirit may move.

And the Spirit of the Lord will come upon thee, and thou shalt prophesy with them, and shalt be turned into another man.

And let it be, when these signs are come unto thee, that thou do as occasion serve thee: for God is with thee.

A man who has had no such hours of inspiration as that which Samuel foretold for Saul, has not enjoyed a full life. He may find the asses which his father has lost, but he will miss the kingdom. It is that kingdom, firmly grounded on political independence and material well-being, which we want to assure for the people of Scotland.

III

What does this mean in practice? It means everywhere, and in all fields, Life and not Death. It means the glory of Scotland resurrected and triumphant in our time. It means that every Scot, wherever he may be, shall feel that his own happiness and success are contributing to Scotland's happiness and success, and shall therefore seek them with a surer determination. He shall feel as his own the triumphs of Scotland in all her spheres, and the joys of all his fellow Scots shall be *his* joys also. It means that we shall be a united people at last.

And what shall be the bond that shall bind us together? Scotland will be the bond, but of that we shall need some visible, tangible symbol. There can be no better symbol than the very earth and heather and rock of our own land. Every man living in Scotland shall know the soil on which he treads to be a part of the uniting bond, and every Scot abroad shall remember and know it too. One crowning symbol—the very same for all—we must all have: and this is the rock round which on Edinburgh Castle, Lorimer built our War Memorial. Beside that rock, rising in the most sacred shrine of our land, let us each silently when we go there promise that, within the measure of our power, we shall make Scotland once more arise and shine with the light of abundant life.

IV

We must absorb the beauty of our own land
until it becomes, not merely something we
externally admire or delight in, but an effec-
tual part of our inmost selves, like the
beauty of the woman we love. How we
should all be thrilled to describe every detail of that beauty if we could find someone
to listen! How much better then to *live* that
beauty, and see it work—through us—upon
the minds and lives of others. Such trans-
forming power is in spiritual love, fired and
hardened by the flame of beauty. We should
make a like use of the natural beauties of
our country, let them impress their outline
deep on our hearts till they become a source
of inspiration within us that nothing can ever
destroy.

If I should tell you of the beauty of my own
glen, you know your own and that is better,
for it means more to you. Your vision is not
the same as mine, and could never be even if

the glen we both knew and cherished in our minds were the same. But the end to which all our visions point is one and the same—it is the rising light of Scotland.

CHAPTER XIII

THE END IN VIEW

' It is not difficult to devise machinery, but no paper plan, however well drafted, is of use if the will to work it is lacking.'

THE RIGHT HON. ANTHONY EDEN, M.P.

WITH EVERY new generation, as with every pair of lovers, the world's great age begins again. But experience has taught us how quickly the dawn of enthusiasm is apt to become overcast by clouds. From whatever airt they blow up, these clouds have all the one effect, they take the spring out of young lives. Let us therefore briefly observe their nature so that we can dismiss them not only from our minds, but also from the Scotland of our sons.

The first great obstacle is the *want of faith* : faith in God and that His will can be done. It is obviously His will that His children should live free and happy, under the shelter of His hills and beside His streams, and not in the hovels of slums. It is no less clearly His will that they should have independent minds and think for themselves on the great questions of life and not be moulded either by dictators or by the mass-machinery of Hollywood and the sensational Press. To destroy these influences altogether is neither possible nor desirable: all that is necessary is that our compatriots shall keep open the gateway of the spirit, and this they can in present circumstances only be sure of doing if they regain touch with Nature. More and more of them must return to the Highlands, there to live off the produce of the land and of the sea.

If the first reason why hopes are often clouded is want of faith, the second is the crude idea—just as common to-day as in Nazareth long ago—that miracles can be achieved at will. The men of Nazareth asked Jesus to perform for them the same miracles as He had done in Capernaum, and He told them that without the co-operation of their faith such miracles were impossible. Democratic peoples like the French and ourselves who always expect to sit aside and watch *the Government* saving them, cannot be saved in that way either. Our co-operation is needed, and not simply the co-operation of talk, the passing of resolutions, the clamour for a comprehensive survey of every aspect of Highland life in every county of the Highlands—with nothing to be *done* until this survey is completed. In one of the Everlasting Heritage talks broadcast last December, Ian Macpherson very sensibly suggested that a beginning should be made with one small area—perhaps the Isle of Mull—to see how the proposed developments would work out in practice.[1] ' We should take strong exception to any such proposal,' re-

[1] The National Trust for Scotland have bought a farm in Mull, and with the co-operation of the West of Scotland Agricultural College and the Pilgrim Trust, are reconditioning it along modern lines as an experiment which may have important results for West Highland agriculture.

plied the Secretary of the Highland Development League. Like an over-cautious commander he must wait till the last drummer-boy has arrived in camp, and by that time the chance for action will have gone.

The two present essentials are first to release the spirit of Scotland and free it for action;[1] secondly and at once to point the way, as Sir John Orr has done above, to a practical and really useful advance not in seven directions, but in one. Let talk stop and work begin, and there will soon be something to talk about.

II

The bracken which encroaches on hill pastures, especially in Central Scotland, is a symbol of the state we have come to. People sometimes wonder how our ancestors managed to deal with bracken: the answer is that

[1] A Scottish Nationalist, to whom I am indebted for many friendly criticisms, would add this rider:

' Certainly, provided *we* have control over the governmental mind (policy) and machine (administration).'

they were not troubled with bracken, because they kept cattle on the hillsides instead. They had a positive policy—to rear cattle: our policy at best is negative, to keep down the bracken. It is because we do not cultivate and make full use of our land that the bracken makes use of it for us. So long as we have merely negative ideas in our heads, we shall get merely negative results. This is true of Scottish life in other directions: it is true of the contrast between hundreds of thousands of men wanting work and a great amount of work needing to be done; it is true of our religious life, which is still occupied with 'Thou shalt not'. The bracken spreading over our hillsides is a sign that we have not the courage or imagination to stand up and live.

Once we decide to develop the land of Scotland, it will be worth making a large-scale attack on the bracken. That would not be difficult. The simplest way to get rid of bracken is to cut it over when the young fronds appear above the ground, and to repeat the process a short time later. If this is done for three years in succession the bracken will be subdued.

A grant is given by the Government to machine-cutting, with the object of ' stimulating modern invention to find out reliable methods for destroying bracken more quickly and more cheaply than by the old and well-understood method of man and scythe '.[1]

It is plain that here, as so often, the Government have taken up a scheme which will help the large man and not the small man, and are blandly pretending that it will help everybody. Bracken-cutting by machine can only be done in fairly flat country, and such land generally belongs to large sheep-farmers who are comparatively prosperous.

It is the hilly districts, usually in the hands of small farmers, that need help most, and a

[1] Lord Strathcona, for the Government, in the House of Lords, 21st July, 1937.

horse drawing an iron bar cannot perform along a steep hillside. Here, therefore, as in the Herring Industry Board's scheme for reconditioning of boats, the Government have produced a scheme that will do no good to the small independent man in Scotland.

A request for a grant towards hand-cutting of bracken was refused on two grounds:

(1) It would cost too much.

(2) It would involve an army of inspectors.

The inspection should be entrusted to the resident laird or (if the laird is not resident) to some responsible individual such as the parish minister or a justice of the peace, who would do it for nothing. We are, indeed, smothered in red tape if this modest revival of the old local government is no longer practicable in the Highlands.

As for the cost of the grant, there is a huge surplus of men and women available for such work in the Highlands. Adult unemployment in Highland and North-east counties last April was as follows:

Caithness and Sutherland	-	39·9%
Ross and Cromarty	- -	55·6%
Inverness-shire	- - -	22%
Argyll	- - - -	25·2%
Nairn	- - - -	23·6%
Moray	- - - -	17·4%
Banffshire	- - - -	41·3%
Aberdeenshire	- - -	15·8%
Angus	- - - -	17·9%
Perthshire	- - - -	9·5%

It would be interesting to work out the cost of these figures in unemployment benefit, and to add to it the cost of keeping land under bracken instead of under sheep: then to subtract from this total the cost of organising up and down the Highlands the camps of the bracken-cutters, who would be extremely well, but inexpensively, fed off country produce as the Government's guests, and be paid in addition the full sum which they would have drawn as unemployed. The men would be volunteers, and all arrangements for transporting them from their home to the Highland camps would be undertaken by the Government.

The mere sight of something happening on so large a scale as this, when successive Secretaries of State for Scotland had gone on saying that ' nothing can be done ' would put life into dry bones from John o' Groats to the Mull of Galloway. It would be particularly appropriate next spring, when we are inviting the world to come to our Empire Exhibition and see what Scotland can do.

The world would indeed be impressed if in the same year as we stage an Empire Exhibition we make a resolute and successful bid to put our own hillsides in order. It would need planning and it would need determination; but it is worth doing and it can be done.

III

The Scots, as we saw in Chapter I, are a people of contraries. They are both more logical and more sentimental than the English: there are for example MacDonalds in the West Highlands to whom the Massacre of Glencoe is to-day a more personal tragedy than the

Great War. No scheme will do any good for
Scotland which does not take account both of
sentiment and logic, as well as of common
sense. Scientific developments, especially
electrical power for true rural industries,
Professor Stapledon's methods of improving
grass land and the Macaulay Institute's experiments with peat, can help Scotland greatly on
her difficult path into a full life. But only a
stranger, or a Scot who has lived so long in
England that he has forgotten what it feels like
to be a Scot, would expect gratitude for offer-
ing to Scotland the full blast of a materialist
civilisation. That civilisation, in any event, is
doomed. It has been built up on a growing
expansion of industrial plant until the urge to
establish new industries and so create employment has become almost a craze in political
circles. When re-armament is over we shall
find that we have many more factories than
there is work to fill them. The numbers of
the unemployed in Britain will become sud-
denly and permanently much larger than even

the large figures of to-day, and a new policy
will be sought in a hurry in order to save the
economic system upon which our present
civilisation is built. The only relief will be,
as the Russians have done, to dilute the
system. Our system is industrial, and we
shall have to make it much more agricultural.
If Sir John Orr's proposals have been successfully carried out in the Highlands, Scotland
will have thrown to her larger neighbour a
life-line just in time.

Not only unemployment, but the problems
of housing and nutrition will both be made
easier when large numbers of Scotsmen have
returned to the land to live there and produce
more food for themselves and the urban population. The full effect of this transfusion
of Scotland's life-blood cannot be measured
by statistics: it would release nation-wide
energies now dormant and unimagined.

But this cannot be begun until the life of
the crofters who are in the Highlands already
has been made more secure and tolerable.

A NEW POLICY

For this purpose legislation will be required, to implement the decisions recently given in local courts against a separate assessment of crofters' dwelling-houses. Crofters have always regarded subsidiary earnings as essential to their existence : formerly such earnings were often derived from the inshore fishing which is at present in decay ; the crofters feel keenly that what they earn by taking in boarders in the holiday season is not to be regarded as an extra, but as part of their ordinary means of livelihood. They have a hard struggle in present conditions, and no re-population of the land on a large scale can be expected until the men and women who are there already are given practical help in such ways as Sir John Orr has suggested.

CHAPTER XIV

CONCLUSION

'But I tell you of a truth, many widows were in Israel in the days of Elias, when the heaven was shut up three years and six months, when great famine was throughout all the land;

'But unto none of them was Elias sent, save unto Sarepta, a city of Sidon, unto a woman that was a widow.

'And many lepers were in Israel in the time of Eliseus the prophet; and none of them was cleansed, saving Naaman the Syrian.'

LUKE IV, 25-27

ALL TRUE religion keeps a window open to welcome destiny, for it has learnt that destiny is not an enemy but a friend. We serve a Purpose beyond ourselves, and what happens to us is not necessarily determined by any merits or demerits of our own; it may happen for some quite accidental reason that suits the particular purpose in hand. Elijah had to be preserved during the years of famine, and a widow's cottage in Sidon was conveniently remote from the wrath of Ahab. Elisha had to manifest Jehovah's powers of healing, and the generalissimo of Israel's late enemy was a spectacular instrument to that purpose.

This is a sane view of life, and perfectly accords with the promise of Christ that each of God's children is precious in His sight: ' ye are of more value than many sparrows,' and ' the very hairs of your head are all numbered.' Indeed, He tells us this at the very moment of urging us not to worry about what will happen to us. The combination of faith in an ultimate Purpose which includes us down to the smallest detail, with a care-free confidence that our own fate in this world is of little moment, is the very goal we should aim at if we want to be ourselves. Just such an assurance must have animated Bruce as he rode out on his little pony to challenge Sir

Henry de Bohun. He knew that the things for which he had striven were not going to fail, whatever might happen to him, and so the challenge seemed to himself a smaller risk than it did to his bewildered followers.

We see the same sublime confidence in Keats.

> If I should die, said I to myself, I have left no immortal work behind me, nothing to make my friends proud of my memory, but I have loved the principle of beauty in all things, and if I had had time, I would have made myself remembered.

What mattered was not that, if he had had time, he would have made himself remembered, but that he had loved the principle of beauty in all things. He had found the Purpose, the Purpose was immortal, and whatever might befall his poems the cause for which he stood was victorious against Time —yes, even if fools should in time destroy every beautiful thing upon the earth.

Men whose faith is of this quality have a power beyond their fellows. Where they seek, they shall find: where they knock, it shall be opened unto them. Let them call now upon the deep hearts of the Scottish people, and they shall find a response that will surprise them.

APPENDIX

HIGHLAND HOME INDUSTRIES

By Miss Jean Bruce, Secretary

1. About 50 to 60 years ago two bodies were formed to help the cottage workers and small local industries in Scotland to find a market for their produce.

  (a) The Scottish Home Industries Association—President, Millicent, Duchess of Sutherland.

  (b) The Co-operative Council of Highland Home Industries, of which body the late Lady Rosebery, the late Dowager Countess of Dunmore and the late Lady Mackenzie of Gairloch were the moving spirits.

The former embraced the whole of Scotland and chiefly concerned itself with the uniting of small existing bodies under one head, *e.g.*, The Sutherland Home Industries, The Crofters Agency, The Fife Handspun Linen Community Lacemaking in Fife, Argyll and Ayrshire, Hand-loom Weavers in the Scottish Borders, etc., etc. The latter confined its energies to the Highlands and Islands and Galloway. In course of time the first body found that home industries were dying out in most parts of Scotland

HIGHLAND HOME INDUSTRIES

except in the Highlands and in 1914 Millicent, Duchess of Sutherland wishing to devote her energies to war work, suggested that the Co-operative Council should carry on her work with the exception of the Sutherland Industries in which she wished to hold the controlling influence.

This was agreed to and the two bodies carried on until 1921 under the name of ' Co-operative Council of Highland Home Industries '. In that year a Company (Limited by Guarantee) was formed under the present title of ' Highland Home Industries Ltd.' Both these bodies were set up because of the exploitation of the crofters in the Highlands and Islands by the system of barter, then the only means of trade in the North. In addition, the crofters used to bring their wares to the Lairds and ask them to find a sale among their friends. It was with the idea of finding a wider market that these Companies were formed.

It was realised that:

(c) A rural population must be preserved.
(d) Crofting alone without subsidiary industries was not sufficient livelihood especially when the crofts were infertile as was often the case especially in the Outer Isles.
(e) That as well as fishing, all home arts such as spinning, knitting, embroidery, weaving, etc., should be encouraged and sales depots should be opened throughout the country.

At its inception several interested friends gave loans amounting to £1000 to start the work. In

293

1911 Mrs. Burnly Campbell, who had organised the Highland Clachan at the Glasgow Exhibition, handed over part of the profits of the Clachan amounting to £1300 to the Company. This sum forms the Capital of the Company.

All goods are bought outright from the makers. There is no 'Sale or Return'. The Company pays cash, giving the worker the highest possible price consistent with the market value of their goods.

All Directors give their services voluntarily and no profits are made by the Company. If there is a balance in hand in any year, it is spent on improving the standard of existing industries or sending teachers to start new industries, etc., etc., e.g. The Company's School of Weaving and Basketmaking in Skye, Rug-making in Lewis, periodic visits to the Highlands and Islands to give new patterns and new ideas so that the products may be as up-to-date as possible.

2. I give here the audited figure of our purchases from all workers for the last six years:

1930 to 1931	£12,938
1931 to 1932	£12,876
1932 to 1933	£13,495
1933 to 1934	£12,944
1934 to 1935	£13,610
1935 to 1936	£15,218
1936 to 1937	£13,434 (A regrettable drop, largely due to overstocking the previous year.)

3. The hard work has chiefly been to raise the standard of work and to keep the workers up-to-date in their productions. This has been done by personal house to house visitation—an arranged meeting is not so effective because the people—mostly women getting on in years—are not accustomed to listen to speeches. The response has been very ready, but some of the workers don't take any criticism of their work very willingly. This is now improved when they find that we will *not* take in any work which does not come up to our specification. At the present time we cannot take all the work we are offered as our purchases are limited to our ready cash and as has already been stated, we are under capitalized.

4. We confine ourselves as far as the Outer Islands are concerned to the handspun, handwoven, vegetable-dyed tweeds as we feel that this type of work spreads the money more, as many spinners (and spinners are far more numerous than weavers) are thrown out of all hope of augmenting their income under the new conditions which now exist at Stornoway. I understand that many more weavers are now employed in Lewis, but if the system were introduced in the other Islands, the number of weavers employed would be small in proportion to the number of hand spinners thrown out of work. The real genuine *handspun* Harris tweed will always be a luxury trade, but the demand for the real stuff is increasing and will, I think, continue to do so.

5. Much as I personally deplore the thought of the

HIGHLAND HOME INDUSTRIES

Highlands being a trippers' paradise, I cannot but confess that the better class tourists are a very profitable source of income and if the right type of tourist could be encouraged, our trade would undoubtedly be helped. In Strathpeffer and Skye together, our total annual sales are in the neighbourhood of £3500.

6. Total number of workers dealt with
   individually   887
   Payment to above 1934-1935   £13,610
   Payment to above 1935-1936   £15,218

INDEX

INDEX

298

INDEX

INDEX

INDEX

INDEX

PRINTED IN GREAT BRITAIN BY ROBERT MACLEHOSE AND CO. LTD.
THE UNIVERSITY PRESS, GLASGOW